JOEL OSTEEN

TODAY I CHOOSE

Devotions for
a Better Life

Today I Choose: Devotions for a Better Life

ISBN: 978-1-963492-62-0

Created and assembled for Joel Osteen Ministries by
Breakfast for Seven
breakfastforseven.com

Printed in China.

TABLE OF CONTENTS

"OH, THAT YOU WOULD

CHOOSE LIFE,

SO THAT YOU AND YOUR

DESCENDANTS

MIGHT LIVE!"

DEUTERONOMY 30:19 NLT

INTRODUCTION

Every day you make choices. *Am I going to get up when the alarm goes off, or am I going to hit snooze? Am I going to have a good attitude as I enter this day, or am I going to grumble and complain? Am I going to spend time in the presence of the Lord, or am I going to use my time on other things?*

Someone will inevitably hurt or annoy you — will you be gracious and forgiving, or will you choose to take offense? Something will happen that will ask you to rise up — will you give in to fear and doubt, or will you choose powerful thinking, focusing on God's promises, and doing it afraid?

If you looked back over your life, you would no doubt discover that you have made some good choices, maybe even great ones. It's likely that you have also made some choices that weren't so good, that didn't turn out so well, perhaps some that you wish you could take back. From the moment we wake up, we are faced with choices — choices that define our lives, shape our relationships, impact our health and our careers, and test our faith. Some choices come easily, while others require courage, determination, and new direction.

No matter where you are in your faith journey, God has given you the right to make choices for your life. *Today I Choose* is a 90-day devotional that reflects that power to choose — to choose the best life God has planned for you, the life that is available to you when you choose to honor Him.

Each day, for the next 90 days, you will be invited to focus on one powerful choice — choices like healing, hope, freedom, authenticity, victory, surrender, and unconditional trust. Along with a guiding scripture, you'll find encouragement from the Bible and through personal stories that will help you apply these choices to your life. These choices may seem small, but when made intentionally, and daily, they can shape your mindset, strengthen your faith, and bring peace to your soul.

God has given you the power to not only choose but to also choose wisely. When you do, watch out — a better life, an abundant life, is in store.

"Today I have given you the choice between life and death, between blessings and curses. Now I call on heaven and earth to witness the choice you make. Oh, that you would choose life, so that you and your descendants might live! You can make this choice by loving the Lord your God, obeying him, and committing yourself firmly to him. This is the key to your life. And if you love and obey the Lord, you will live long in the land the Lord swore to give your ancestors Abraham, Isaac, and Jacob."

Deuteronomy 30:19–20 (NLT)

TODAY I CHOOSE

To See Myself as God Sees Me

Even before he made the world, God loved us and chose us in Christ to be holy and without fault in his eyes.
Ephesians 1:4 (NLT)

God didn't make any of us to be average. He didn't make us to barely get by. We were created to excel. Before the foundation of the world, God chose us, loved us, and equipped us with everything we would need to live an abundant life with Him.

You have seeds of greatness on the inside of you right now, but it's up to you to believe it and act on it. You will never rise above the image that you have of yourself, and that's why it's so important that we see ourselves as God sees us.

Every day you should make positive declarations over your life. Say things like: "I am blessed. I am prosperous. I am healthy. I am talented. I am creative. I am wise." When we do that, we build up our self-image into the image God has of us. Those words are going to get down on the inside and eventually they'll begin to change the way we see ourselves. Say what God says about you: "I am a new creation. I'm forgiven. I'm valuable to God. He has made me worthy" (2 Corinthians 5:17–21; 1 John 1:9; Isaiah 43:4). Keep saying that long enough, and you'll start expecting good things.

Some of you have probably had other people speak negative, destructive words over you. Unfortunately, you've heard those words so many times that it has affected your self-image. The only way that's going to change is for you to get on the offensive and start speaking faith-filled words over your life. The best eraser you can ever find for negative words is God's Word. Quit dwelling on what others have said and start saying out of your own mouth what God says about you: "I am anointed. I am approved. I am equipped. I've been chosen. I've been set apart. I am destined to live in victory" (1 John 2:27; Romans 15:7; 2 Timothy 3:16–17; 1 Peter 2:9; 1 Corinthians 15:57). When you do that, you bless your life.

Today I choose to see myself as God sees me. I am chosen. I am loved. I am a victor and not a victim. God has equipped me for the good plan He has for my life.

TODAY I CHOOSE

To Reprogram My Thinking

You will keep in perfect peace all who trust in you, all whose thoughts are fixed on you!
Isaiah 26:3 (NLT)

When I stepped up to pastor the church after my father died, every thought told me, *You can't do this, Joel. You don't know how to minister. You don't have the experience. Nobody is going to come.* It would have been easy to let those thoughts take root and keep me from my destiny.

One Sunday, right after I first started, I was in the lobby after service, and I overheard two ladies talking. One said, "He's not as good as his father." The other said, "I don't think he's going to make it." I was already intimidated and insecure and didn't think I could do it, and now the enemy was trying to use others to add to my fears.

My first thought was to panic. My worst fears were coming true. But then something rose up in me, and I thought, *Those ladies don't determine my destiny. They don't know what God has put in me. They didn't call me, they didn't equip me, they didn't anoint me, and more than anything else, they don't have the final say; God does. And He says I'm well able and strong in the Lord. I can do all things through Christ.*

I had to reprogram my thinking. Just like a computer has a delete button, I had to hit delete on all those negative voices, including the ones in my own head! When my thoughts said, *You can't do it,* I hit delete. When my thoughts said, *People will quit coming to church,* I hit delete. When my thoughts said, *You aren't qualified,* I hit delete. When those ladies said I wasn't going to make it, I hit delete. The thoughts kept coming back for a while, but I kept hitting delete.

You can dwell on every negative thing people have said and every fear that comes to your own mind, or you can choose to delete it all and fix your thoughts on God. I promise you this: I wouldn't be doing what I am doing today if I hadn't reprogrammed my thinking.

> *Today I choose to reprogram my thinking. God has the final say, and He says I can do all things through Christ.*

TODAY I CHOOSE

To Be Happy

Happy are the people who are in such a state;
happy are the people whose God is the LORD*!*
Psalm 144:15 (NKJV)

I remember playing basketball with a young man who was always in a good mood. He was so friendly and upbeat all the time. One day after our game, I asked if he wanted to go get something to eat. He said he couldn't because he had to go to the clinic for his chemotherapy appointment.

He went on to tell me he had been fighting cancer for three years. I was shocked. I didn't know anything was wrong. I said, "I'm so sorry to hear that." And he responded, "Don't feel sorry for me. Life is good. I'm blessed. I have a beautiful wife and a new son. I am grateful to be alive."

He could have been depressed. He could have asked, "Why me?" and complained, "Life isn't fair!" He could have stayed home, wallowing in self-pity. Instead, he made the choice to be happy and to feel blessed.

I asked him how he could have such a great attitude. He said, "When I wake up in the morning, I ask myself: *Do I want to live depressed, or do I want to live happy?* I choose to live happy."

David said in Psalm 144:15, *Happy are the people whose God is the* LORD (NKJV). The reason we can be happy is not because faith keeps us from trouble and bad breaks. The reason we can be happy is because God is on the throne. He controls the universe. He is our Provider, our Healer, our Vindicator, and our Way Maker. We can be happy that the most powerful force in the universe is on our side. We can be happy that what was meant for harm He is turning to our advantage (Genesis 50:20). We can be happy that He promised to work out His plan for our lives (Jeremiah 29:11). We can be happy that all the forces of darkness cannot stop what God has ordained for us. We can be happy about that!

Today I choose to be happy. God is greater than my circumstances, and because He has given me the authority to choose how I want to live my life, I choose to be happy!

TODAY I CHOOSE

To Have Patient Endurance

Patient endurance is what you need now, so that you will continue to do God's will. Then you will receive all that he has promised.
Hebrews 10:36 (NLT)

We're all waiting for something — waiting for a dream to come to pass, our health to improve, or a child to turn around. The longer we wait without seeing anything happening, the easier it gets to be discouraged and think that it's not meant to be. But I want to tell you: Don't get talked out of what God put in your heart. Just because it hasn't happened yet doesn't mean it is not going to happen.

God is faithful, and what you are believing for is on the way. God is working behind the scenes right now, lining up the right people and arranging the good breaks, the healing, the freedom, and the abundance.

But what you do while you're waiting will determine whether you see the promise. That's why God said you need *patient endurance* — not just patience, but endurance. That means you aren't going to be talked out of it. You are going to keep thanking God when you don't see any sign. You're going to keep believing when every circumstance says there's no way. When others get what you are waiting for, you are going to praise God for it and say, "You did it for them; I know You'll do it for me." When you do that, God says you will receive ALL that He has promised — not some, not a little, not most, but ALL of it — the fullness of the blessing.

You may be in a waiting season now, but don't let delays convince you to lower your expectations. God put that dream in you because He has every intention of bringing it to pass.

In Psalm 5:3, David wrote, *Listen to my voice in the morning, Lord. Each morning I bring my requests to you and wait expectantly* (NLT). Wait expectantly. Wait in faith. Wait with gratitude, knowing that God is working and what you are waiting for is coming. Wait with patient endurance.

We're all going to wait, but how we wait makes all the difference.

Today I choose to have patient endurance. I will not be discouraged. I will wait in faith until I receive all that God has promised me.

TODAY I CHOOSE

To Have a Good Mood

This is the day the L*ORD has made; we will rejoice and be glad in it.*
Psalm 118:24 (NKJV)

God created us as emotional beings. We can feel joy, excitement, and passion; and we can also feel sorrow, sadness, and discouragement. When you wake up in the morning, you can feel gloomy and irritated. But then after you've had a cup of coffee, you feel better, more energetic and positive about the day ahead. That's because feelings come and go, and they can change on a dime. The mistake we make is when we let feelings determine our moods.

Psalm 118 says, *We will rejoice.* Your will is more powerful than your feelings. Say to discouragement, "I will rejoice." Say to self-pity, "I will be glad." Say to doubt, "I will have faith!" Say to negativity, "You don't control me; today I choose a good mood!"

Living by our feelings is a very surface-level way of living. You have to go deeper than that. You can't stop the feelings from coming, but you don't have to get on board with them. You can live this day in faith. You can choose what kind of day this is.

How you start your day makes all the difference. The enemy works overtime every morning to try to set a negative tone for your day. Instead of letting him set the tone, start the day in faith. Before your feet hit the floor in the morning, you can decide that it is going to be a good day, and you are going to live it in faith.

Scripture says that *joy comes with the morning* (Psalm 30:5, NLT). Every morning, joy is waiting for you. God sends it just for you. But the enemy sends all those other feelings — guilt, shame, sadness, and anger. So, you have to choose. If you are going to live a victorious life, if you are going to reach your full potential, then choose a good mood despite your feelings!

Don't wait for the good feelings to come. Get your mind on the right thoughts, and the feelings will eventually follow.

Today I choose to have a good mood.
I do not live by my feelings;
I live by faith.

TODAY I CHOOSE

To Be a Safe Place

When they kept on questioning him, he straightened up and said to them, "Let any one of you who is without sin be the first to throw a stone at her."
John 8:7 (NIV)

We live in a culture filled with judgment. People are quick to assume without knowing all the facts. They gossip, spread rumors, cast shame, and try to discredit people. They are throwing stones.

But as Christians, we aren't called to throw stones. We are called to lift the fallen, to restore the broken, and to heal the hurting. People don't need more judgment — they have enough people beating them down — they need someone to lift them up. This isn't about approving of someone's sins; this is about loving someone back to wholeness. You are never more like God than you are when you are helping people in need.

In the Old Testament, they operated under the "eye for an eye" law, meaning that if you killed someone, you, too, would be killed. But God told Joshua to set up six cities that would be known as cities of refuge (Joshua 20:2). Regardless of what you did, if you made it to the city of refuge, you would be spared. The people there would protect you and keep you from harm. This is a picture of what happened to all of us. We were born into sin, made mistakes, and deserved judgment. But Jesus came as our Refuge. He is our Safe Place. When we come to Him, we don't receive the judgment we deserve. We receive mercy, forgiveness, and new beginnings.

Jesus said in Matthew, *"Freely you have received; freely give"* (Matthew 10:8, NIV). You have received all this mercy; now freely give it away. Others should know they can come to you and not be looked down on — that you don't have stones of judgment or condemnation to throw. You have the oil of forgiveness and understanding that will help them get back on their feet.

Today I choose to be a safe place. I will not cast judgment. God has freely given me grace, mercy, and forgiveness, so I will be generous and give grace to others.

TODAY I CHOOSE

To Try Again

The godly may trip seven times, but they will get up again. But one disaster is enough to overthrow the wicked.
Proverbs 24:16 (NLT)

We've all tried something that didn't work out — tried to start a business, tried to have a baby, tried to lose the weight, tried rehab, tried to forgive. We did our best, but our best didn't seem good enough. We weren't able to do it. We weren't able to succeed.

If you aren't prayerful, that failure can set you back and make you not want to try again. *The relationship didn't work; I don't want to get hurt again. My boss said I wasn't qualified; I don't want to get rejected again. I tried to make peace with my loved one; I only made it worse. I tried to forgive, but it was just too hard.* Just because it hasn't happened yet doesn't mean it's not going to happen. The people who reach their destiny are the people who try again.

God has a window of grace for you, where He will empower you to do what you couldn't do before. He will give you favor that causes doors to open and the right people to show up. He'll give you an anointing of ease where there used to be a struggle. You have the grace to forgive, the grace to get healthy, the grace to take new ground. But this power, this window of grace, is only activated if you try again.

The enemy would love for you to give up, to live disappointed, to think that it's too late. But this setback isn't a surprise to God. For every setback, He's already planned a comeback. For every loss, He has a new beginning. For every closed door, He has an open door. We are all going to fail at times, but the question is: Are you going to get back up? Are you going to believe that God still has a good plan for your life? Are you going to believe that what He started He will finish? Are you going to try again?

Today I choose to try again.
This failure isn't final.
Success is in my future.

TODAY I CHOOSE

To Do It God's Way

"My thoughts are nothing like your thoughts,"
says the Lord. *"And my ways are far*
beyond anything you could imagine."
Isaiah 55:8 (NLT)

Naaman was a captain in the Syrian army. He was a very influential, well-respected man, but he had leprosy, an incurable disease. A young maid that worked for him told him if he'd go see the prophet Elisha in Israel, Elisha would heal him.

Naaman took her advice. He traveled a great distance and announced his arrival at Elisha's house. But when Elisha heard Naaman was there, he didn't go out to meet him. He didn't even offer to pray for him. He sent his servant to tell Naaman to wash seven times in the Jordan River and he would be healed.

Offended, Naaman stormed off and said: "*I thought he would certainly come out to meet me!" he said. "I expected him to wave his hand over the leprosy and call on the name of the* Lord *his God and heal me!*" (2 Kings 5:11, NLT).

Naaman had a preconceived idea of how God was going to heal him. He thought Elisha would come out. He expected him to wave his hand over him and say a healing prayer. And when God didn't do it the way he expected, Naaman almost walked away from his miracle.

You can't put God in a box. He may not turn that problem around in a traditional way. He may not bring your dream to pass in the way you expect Him to. Just because He did it that way for your friend doesn't mean He will do it the same way for you. Just because He answered your prayer that way once doesn't mean He'll answer in the same way the next time. Stay open and let God do it His way.

Naaman's assistant convinced him to try it God's way. Naaman went down to the Jordan River and washed seven times. After the seventh time, he was completely healed. Here's my point: the healing wasn't in the water, or he would have been healed the first time. The healing was in his willingness to do it God's way.

Today I choose to do it God's way.
I trust that His way is higher!

TODAY I CHOOSE

To Receive God's Grace

But he said to me, "My grace is sufficient for you, for my power is made perfect in weakness." Therefore I will boast all the more gladly about my weaknesses, so that Christ's power may rest on me.
2 Corinthians 12:9 (NIV)

The apostle Paul had what he called *a thorn in my flesh* (2 Corinthians 12:7, NIV). The scripture doesn't tell us exactly what his *thorn* was, but it was something that bothered him, something physical or emotional that he didn't like. It may have been painful or simply annoying. Perhaps he felt like it was hindering his ministry and all that God called him to do and to preach. So, he prayed for God to take it away: *Three times I pleaded with the Lord to take it away from me* (v. 8, NIV). But God didn't remove the thorn from his life.

Paul was fulfilling his purpose. God had chosen him, and Paul was delivering. He wrote half the books in the New Testament. He was sold out for Christ. You would think God would fix what was bothering him. But instead of removing it, God said to him, *"My grace is sufficient for you"* (v. 9, NIV).

God was saying, "I'm not going to remove it, at least not yet, but I will give you the grace to handle it. I will give you the strength to do what I am calling you to do. I will give you grace to be where you are with a good attitude so that you can enjoy your life, even with this hindrance, because My grace is enough. Do you receive it?"

Later, in his letter to the Philippians, Paul wrote: *I have learned the secret of being content* (Philippians 4:12, NIV). It didn't happen automatically. He learned it. He chose it. He received God's grace for any and every situation, and that allowed him to be relaxed, happy, and comfortable.

Whatever your thorn is, God has grace for it. Whatever it is you want Him to change that He's not changing, He wants to give you grace for it. Like Paul, you can choose to be happy where you are — trouble and all, sickness and all, loneliness and all, thorn and all.

Today I choose to receive God's grace. His grace is all I need.

TODAY I CHOOSE

To Increase

"So I have come down to rescue them from the power of the Egyptians and lead them out of Egypt into their own fertile and spacious land. It is a land flowing with milk and honey. . . ."
Exodus 3:8 (NLT)

For forty years, as the Israelites wandered in the desert, the one thing they could always count on was manna. Every morning, like clockwork, God provided their daily bread. They knew that was the hand of God taking care of them. What they didn't realize was that the manna was only temporary provision. God had more for them. He was taking them into *a land flowing with milk and honey*. When they got close to this land, the scripture says *the manna ceased* (Joshua 5:12, NKJV). The NLT version says *it was never seen again*.

After forty years of having manna, over twelve thousand mornings, now it was nowhere to be found. I can imagine them panicking: "God, what's happening? You've brought us this far. Why are You leaving us now? Why won't You provide anymore?"

We can be tempted to think the same way when God removes something or someone from our lives. Maybe your best friend moves away, a loved one goes to Heaven, you are laid off, or you are forced to move. *Why is this happening?* It is happening because God is positioning you for increase. It is happening because God knows you will never reach for more if He keeps providing you with manna. It is happening because He has to get you out of your comfort zone.

It wasn't a coincidence that the manna stopped when the Israelites were about to enter the Promised Land. God doesn't stop things unless He has greater provision on the way. When something ceases, it's an indication that increase is coming.

Don't give up on your dreams when the manna ceases. Believe that God is positioning you for increase. Believe that God is in control, His plans for you are good, and He is about to open even bigger doors for you. Believe that your promised land — your healing, your breakthrough, your promotion, your spouse, your next great opportunity — is on its way.

Today I choose to increase. I choose to believe that God uses closed doors to propel us to our destiny.

TODAY I CHOOSE

To Forgive

Then Peter came to him and asked, "Lord, how often should I forgive someone who sins against me? Seven times?" "No, not seven times," Jesus replied, "but seventy times seven!"
Matthew 18:21–22 (NLT)

Peter was known to be hot-tempered and easily offended. He cursed and cut off ears, and Jesus regularly had to put him in his place. But Peter was obviously trying to change, to grow in this area, because he came to Jesus and asked, *"Master, how many times do I forgive a brother or sister who hurts me? Seven?"* (v. 21, MSG). Jewish law said three times, so Peter was willing to more than double that. He probably thought Jesus would applaud him, but Jesus answered instead, *"Seven! Hardly. Try seventy times seven"* (v. 22, MSG).

It wasn't really about the number. Jesus was showing us a principle. He was saying, "I want you to live in a continual process of forgiveness." Jesus knew that every day we would have the opportunity to be hurt, to be offended, to be disappointed, and He wants us to be quick to let those things go, quick to forgive, and quick to move on in our hearts and our minds. If we're not quick to forgive, those offenses can take root.

In the Lord's Prayer, Jesus taught us to pray: *"Give us today our daily bread"* (Matthew 6:11, NIV) and *"forgive us our sins, as we have forgiven those who sin against us"* (Matthew 6:12 NLT). Forgiveness is not something we should do every once in a while. Forgiveness is part of our daily bread. On a daily basis, God is forgiving us, and we should be extending that same forgiveness to others.

How much time are you spending offended, bitter, and holding a grudge? How much more could you accomplish if you started forgiving quickly? How much better would your relationships be if you let go of what people said, forgave the person who did you wrong, and quit reliving the hurts?

Today, and every day, I choose to forgive. Forgiveness is part of my life. I am quick to let things go. I will not live in offense. I am moving forward.

TODAY I CHOOSE

To Rest from My Enemies

During those peaceful years, he was able to build up the fortified towns throughout Judah. No one tried to make war against him at this time, for the L*ORD* *was giving him rest from his enemies.*
2 Chronicles 14:6 (NLT)

In 2 Chronicles 14, King Abijah died, and his son, Asa, became the new king of Israel. Asa inherited a land that was filled with idols, pagan shrines, and monuments to many gods. But the scripture says, *Asa did what was pleasing and good in the sight of the* L*ORD* *his God* (v. 2, NLT). He wasn't going to walk in his father's compromising footsteps. Asa *removed the foreign altars and the pagan shrines. He smashed the sacred pillars and cut down the Asherah poles. He commanded the people of Judah to seek the* L*ORD*, *the God of their ancestors, and to obey his law and his commands* (vv. 3–4, NLT).

Asa was serious about his role as leader of God's chosen people. He refused to let them get away with their idol worship. And because of Asa's faithfulness, the Lord gave him rest from his enemies (v. 6).

If you want rest from your enemies, you'll have to get rid of everything that isn't pleasing to God. You'll have to get rid of all the wrong, negative attitudes and mindsets that surround you. You'll have to get rid of depression, anxiety, insecurity, and fear. You'll have to get rid of anger and unforgiveness. You'll have to stop being content with where you are and start believing that God wants to take you higher.

During his season of rest from his enemies, Asa didn't sit around, wasting time. He knew that peace wouldn't last forever, so he prepared himself and Judah for when their enemies would once again come against them. They built fortified towns and armed themselves with shields and spears (2 Chronicles 14:7–8). In the same way, Ephesians 6 tells us to *put on the full armor of God so that when the enemy strikes, you may be able to stand your ground* (v. 13, NIV). In seasons of rest, we should build up our faith and put on our spiritual armor by praying, reading the Word, and praising God.

Today I choose to rest from my enemies. I will get rid of what doesn't please God, put on the full armor of God, and trust in Him alone.

TODAY I CHOOSE

To Focus on What I Do Have

"How much bread do you have?" he asked.
"Go and find out." They came back and reported,
"We have five loaves of bread and two fish."
Mark 6:38 (NLT)

In Mark 6, a great crowd had followed Jesus to a remote area to hear Him teach. It was getting late in the day, so the disciples said to Jesus, *"Send the people away so that they can . . . buy themselves something to eat"* (v. 36, NIV). But Jesus responded, *"You give them something to eat"* (v. 37, NIV).

The disciples were incredulous. There were five thousand men, plus women and children. *"It would cost a small fortune to feed all these thousands of hungry people,"* they told Jesus (v. 37, TPT).

"How much bread do you have?" Jesus asked. They took a quick inventory. *"We have five loaves of bread and two fish"* (v. 38, NLT). In John's telling of this story, he adds, *"But what are they among so many?"* (John 6:9, NKJV).

It was a logical question. What good are five loaves of bread and two fish when thousands of people are hungry? But choice. But the good news is, God has given us the power to keep calm no matter what comes our way.

Jesus said in Luke 17:1, *"It is impossible that no offenses should come"* (NKJV). Offenses will come! That's a promise! The Passion Translation says, *"Betrayals are inevitable."* Inevitable. Unavoidable. You can count on it! Jesus is very clear. He tells us that opportunities to get offended will come, but just because the opportunity is there doesn't mean we have to take the bait.

Don't fall into the trap. People can't make you angry and frustrated; it's your choice. People can't steal your joy and make you unhappy; it's your choice. Make a decision that no matter what happens today, you won't take the bait. With the power that God has given you, you can choose to remain calm regardless of your circumstances.

Today I choose to remain calm. Nothing is going to steal my joy today. I am deciding ahead of time that I will keep my peace.

TODAY I CHOOSE

To Fight for My Future

"The Lord came to him, saying, 'I am the God of your fathers—the God of Abraham, the God of Isaac, and the God of Jacob.'"
Acts 7:31–32 (NKJV)

There are a dozen places in Scripture that refer to "the God of Abraham, Isaac, and Jacob." Abraham is the father of our faith. Isaac was extremely obedient, even willing to be sacrificed. But Jacob was a cheater and a deceiver. He stole his brother's birthright and had to run away to save his own life. Even his name, Jacob, means "supplanter," or "one who takes what isn't rightfully his." Yet Jacob's name is included in this title of God.

Later in his life, Jacob changed his ways. He got his life straightened out, and God sent him back home. Along the way, Jacob wrestled with God. Jacob said to God, *"I am not worthy of all the unfailing love and faithfulness you have shown to me, your servant"* (Genesis 32:10, NLT). And God said to him, "Okay, then let me go," but Jacob said, *"I will not let you go unless you bless me"* (v. 26, NLT).

Jacob knew he was unworthy. He knew he didn't deserve God's kindness. He knew he had stolen his brother's blessing in the past. But he also knew what God — the God of his fathers, Abraham and Isaac — had promised was his inheritance, too. And so he fought. He fought for his future, and he refused to let go until the blessing was rightfully his.

God responded by saying, *"Your name will no longer be Jacob. From now on you will be called Israel, because you have fought with God and with men and have won"* (v. 28, NLT). God changed his name from Jacob to Israel to signify his new beginning and his willingness to fight for his future.

So, why wasn't God known as the God of Abraham, Isaac, and Israel? I think God left it as Abraham, Isaac, and Jacob on purpose to forever settle that no matter what you've done or how far you have fallen, He is your God, too. Your future is promised, but you must be willing to fight for it and to believe that it's yours.

Today I choose to fight for my future.
My God has a good plan for my life.

TODAY I CHOOSE

To Look Again

Jesus put his hands over the man's eyes a second time and made him look up. The man opened his eyes wide and he could see everything perfectly. His eyesight was completely restored!
Mark 8:25 (TPT)

In Mark 8, some people brought a blind man to Jesus and asked Him to heal the man. Jesus put His saliva on the man's eyes and asked him if he could see anything. The man said, "Yes, I can see, but it's not clear." He described what he saw: *"I'm beginning to see people, but they look like trees—walking trees"* (v. 24, TPT). Then, *Jesus put his hands over the man's eyes a second time and made him look up* (v. 25, TPT). This time his vision was perfectly clear.

It's significant that Jesus' first attempt at healing the man didn't heal him completely. It's not like Jesus didn't have enough power that day; it's not like He'd made a mistake. Jesus healed people all the time, but this is the one time that Scripture tells us it took a second time.

After spitting on the man's eyes the first time, Jesus already knew that his vision wasn't clear. He was testing the man. Would he be satisfied with blurred, partial vision?

God doesn't ask you what you *don't* have, and He doesn't ask you to figure out how it's going to happen. He just asks you to look at what you *do* have, what He's already given you, and to trust Him with that. God is so big; He can take what seems small and make something great out of it.

Notice that when Jesus asked the disciples how much bread they had, they came back and not only told Him how many loaves they had but also how many fish. The truth is, you have more than you think you do. When you focus on what you *do* have, God will enlarge your vision. You will see that you're not lacking; He has already placed in you everything you need.

You know how the story ends. When the disciples gave Jesus the five loaves and two fish, there was enough to feed all the people with plenty leftover, because when you put what you have in God's hands, He can multiply it and make it more than enough.

Today I choose to focus on what I do have. God has given me everything I need.

TODAY I CHOOSE

To Believe I Am Who God Says I Am

"Before I formed you in the womb I knew you,
before you were born I set you apart;
I appointed you as a prophet to the nations."
Jeremiah 1:5 (NIV)

The Scriptures tell us that God called Jeremiah to be a prophet to the nations. Jeremiah was young, unsure of himself. He'd never spoken in front of anyone before. But God said to Jeremiah, "Before you showed up on this earth, I already knew everything about you. I knew every weakness you would have and every strength. I knew every bad break that would come your way and all the times you would receive My favor. I knew every person who would do you wrong, and I've set up encouragers to help you along the way. I've already calculated all that into My plan for your life."

Regardless of what others say about you; regardless of your circumstances, your past, or your mistakes; regardless of your age or your experience, God says you are well able. He equipped you and empowered you for your calling before you were ever conceived in your mother's womb.

People may tell you, "You're a mess," but God says He has washed you white as snow (Isaiah 1:18). People may say, "You're a mistake," but God says you are His masterpiece, fearfully and wonderfully made (Ephesians 2:10; Psalm 139:14). People may say, "You're a failure," but God says you're redeemed and His mercy is greater than your mistakes (Psalm 103:4). People may tell you that it's too late for you, but God says His blessings are never late; they are always right on time (Isaiah 60:22). People may tell you that you're worthless, but they don't have the authority to name you or your future — only God does, and He says you are a new creation and an heir to His throne (2 Corinthians 5:17; Romans 8:17).

Get your mind, your words, and your vision going in the right direction. You are who God says you are. You are blessed, you are strong, you are talented, you are prosperous, you are forgiven, you are healthy, you are victorious, you are created in His image, you are a child of the Most High God.

Today I choose to believe I am who God says I am and I can do what He says I can do.

TODAY I CHOOSE

To Pray Boldly

He said, "You're my son, and today is your birthday. What do you want? Name it: Nations as a present? continents as a prize?"
Psalm 2:8 (MSG)

When was the last time you asked God to do something that seemed impossible, out of the ordinary, that you couldn't accomplish on your own? If God answered everything you were praying for right now, would it be big enough? Would you be satisfied? Would He?

Many prayers are not being answered simply because they're not being prayed. If you only pray small prayers, you're not going to see the greatness of our God. If you only ask for little things, you're not going to reach the fullness of your destiny. Psalm 2:8 says that God wants to give you nations as a present, continents as a prize. Are you praying for nations? Are you praying for continents? Or are you praying for just enough to get by?

James 4:3 says, *You ask and do not receive, because you ask amiss* (NKJV). The word *amiss* in the original Greek means "sick, weak, miserable." God isn't interested in sick, weak, miserable prayers. He wants big, bold, nation-sized prayers.

In Joshua 10, the Israelites were fighting against the Amorites, but it was getting late in the day. Joshua could have prayed a weak prayer: "God, help us get home and get a good night's sleep." He could have prayed a miserable prayer: "God, that's good enough. We'll finish them off another time." But Joshua chose to pray a bold prayer. He stood in front of all his people, raised his hands to God, and prayed: *"Sun, stand still"* (v. 12, NKJV). God honored that big, bold prayer, and for twenty-four hours, the sun stayed right where it was so Joshua and his men could finish the job.

When you pray bold prayers, you will see God do supernatural things. He can bring favor, increase, and healing beyond your wildest imagination. He put those impossible dreams in your heart — to build an orphanage, to find a cure, to start your own business, to travel the world — so He can show you that nothing is impossible with Him!

Today I choose to pray bold prayers.
Bold prayers get bold results!

TODAY I CHOOSE

To Speak Healing Words

Kind words heal and help;
cutting words wound and maim.
Proverbs 15:4 (MSG)

It is amazing what one kind word can do. Our words have the power to lift people up, to help them get through a challenge, to encourage them not to give up, and to push them toward their destiny. When you tell someone, "I love you; I'm proud of you; you did a great job on that project," you're not just being kind. Those are healing words. We never know what people are going through, but everyone is going through something; therefore, everyone needs your kindness.

Look at who God has placed in your life: your family, your friends, your coworkers, the clerk at the grocery store, the attendant where you buy gas, the same face you see every time you go to the gym, the person next to you at church, the bank teller, your children's teacher, the guy who shows up to fix your air conditioner, the woman who answers the phone when you call to ask why your bill is so high. They're not there by accident. They need what you have — encouragement, affirmation, gentleness, and kindness. They need to know you believe in them, that you appreciate them, that you see them.

Don't keep the healing to yourself. Be free with your kind words, your compliments, and your encouragement. A blessing is not a blessing until it's spoken. My parents taught us this when we were growing up. When it was one of our birthdays, they had us go around the table and everyone had to say something nice about the person whose birthday it was. This was a way to encourage that person, but it was also to teach us the value of speaking healing words — not just thinking to ourselves what we liked about the person but verbalizing those words so that they could bring healing.

When a kind word comes to your mind, speak it. God would not have put that thought in your mind if He didn't want you to speak it. Don't discount it. Don't talk yourself out of it. You may not even know the person, but God knows what He's doing. There's a reason. They need your healing.

Today I choose to speak healing words. When a kind word comes to my mind, I will speak it.

TODAY I CHOOSE

Calling Over Comfort

But the angel said, "Don't be afraid, Zechariah! God has heard your prayer. Your wife, Elizabeth, will give you a son, and you are to name him John."
Luke 1:13 (NLT)

Zechariah's wife, Elizabeth, had been barren for many years. The couple had prayed and believed for a child in the early days of their marriage, but now they were old. And yet, here the angel was, telling Zechariah that God had heard his prayer and was about to answer it.

Zechariah responded to the angel's miraculous announcement with doubt: *"How can I be sure this will happen? I'm an old man now, and my wife is also well along in years"* (Luke 1:18, NLT). You have to wonder: how many years had gone by since Zechariah had last prayed that prayer for a child, since he'd last believed that God would answer the desires of his heart?

When you have prayed and believed and it hasn't happened, it is easy to settle for where you are, and what you have, rather than to keep believing for more. It is easy to doubt that the answer will come, and, too often, we get comfortable with mediocrity rather than continuing to believe the calling that God has placed on our lives and in our hearts.

Maybe you've been single a long time. You don't think you'll ever meet the right person. That's a season; it's not the end. God has a divine connection already lined up for you. Maybe you feel stuck in your career. You can't seem to get a break. That's not permanent; it's temporary. There is promotion in your future. Maybe you're content with the size of your ministry, even though God has spoken to you about enlarging your tents. He's asking you to choose calling over comfort; He's asking you to get uncomfortable and to keep believing for more.

Don't get comfortable with less than all that God has for you. In fact, be willing to get uncomfortable in order to achieve His calling for you. He may ask you to keep praying, to keep speaking, to keep believing longer than you think you can, but eventually — at just the right time — God will answer your prayers.

Today I choose calling over comfort. I will keep praying and keep believing for all that God has for me.

TODAY I CHOOSE

To Be Grateful

Be thankful in all circumstances, for this is God's will for you who belong to Christ Jesus.
1 Thessalonians 5:18 (NLT)

Far too many people have developed a habit of being negative and complaining in all circumstances. But the Bible tells us to *be thankful in all circumstances*, to be grateful no matter what. You can choose to find things, on purpose, to be grateful for!

While you are getting ready in the morning, you can say: "Lord, thank You for this day!" While driving to work: "Lord, thank You for my job and for this car to get me there." While having lunch: "Lord, thank You for my health." While driving home in the evening, "Lord, thank You for my family and my house."

Unfortunately, it is easy to think about what is wrong. It takes very little effort to turn your mind to the negative — the job you don't like, the neighbor who gets on your nerves, the traffic that is always too heavy, the kids who are wearing you out, and the dishes that need done. Instead, we need to intentionally meditate on God's goodness at all times. We need to choose to be grateful.

When you get stuck in traffic, instead of complaining, you can say, "Lord, thank You for directing my steps. I know I am at the right place at the right time." When your child is causing you heartache, instead of worrying about everything that could go wrong, say: "Lord, thank You that as for me and my house, we will serve You. The seed of the righteous will be mighty in the land." When you get a negative medical report, say: "Lord, thank You that You are my Healer. Nothing can snatch me out of Your hands."

It's not enough to just go to church on Sunday. That won't keep you filled with enough gratitude to get you through the week. It might not even be enough to get you through the day! Instead, you have to choose to be grateful at all times, in all circumstances, every hour of every day. This is God's will for you, and, because it is His will, it is possible!

Today I choose to be grateful. I believe that I will always have something to be thankful for!

TODAY I CHOOSE

To Remember

"But don't be afraid of them! Just remember what the LORD your God did to Pharaoh and to all the land of Egypt. Remember the great terrors the LORD your God sent against them. You saw it all with your own eyes! And remember the miraculous signs and wonders, and the strong hand and powerful arm with which he brought you out of Egypt. The LORD your God will use this same power against all the people you fear."

Deuteronomy 7:18–19 (NLT)

After God rescued the Israelites out of Egypt, they still had plenty of battles ahead of them. But each time one of those battles came, God said, "Don't be afraid. Remember how I showed up for you in the past. I did it before, and I will do it again."

Like the Israelites, each one of us has seen God show up in our lives. He promoted you, gave you that good break; things fell into place. He gave you strength when you didn't think you could go on. That wasn't a lucky break. That was the hand of God. He made a way when you didn't see a way. You didn't like the difficulty, but God got you through it. And now you have a history with Him.

That history is there to encourage you the next time you face a challenge. When you have a setback in your health, a relationship that sours, or a deal at work that falls through, you don't have to get negative and discouraged. You can remember how God brought you out of that trouble — how He protected you, promoted you, and restored you. Faith will rise up in you, and you will know: "God did it for me once; He'll do it for me again. He made a way in the past; He'll make a way in the future." Every challenge you come through victoriously will be the fuel you need to get you through the next one if you choose to remember all that He has done.

Today I choose to remember.
God did miracles in my past,
and I expect Him to do miracles
again in my future.

TODAY I CHOOSE

To Declare Favor

Surely goodness and mercy shall follow me all the days of my life, and I shall dwell in the house of the Lord *forever.*
Psalm 23:6 (ESV)

The word *goodness* in Psalm 23 can be translated as "favor." So, when David wrote, *Surely goodness and mercy shall follow me all the days of my life,* in effect, he was saying, "Favor is keeping my enemies from defeating me. Favor is bringing opportunity and promotion. God's favor is continually on me." He didn't just think it. He didn't just hope it would all work out. He declared favor over his life.

No wonder the prophet Samuel came looking for David to anoint as king. No wonder David defeated a giant twice his size. No wonder King Saul couldn't kill him. When you're constantly declaring the favor of God, you're going to overcome obstacles that look insurmountable and go places you couldn't go on your own.

When I was growing up, there were five of us children, and we never left for school without Mother saying, "Father, thank You that my children have Your favor." It's good to pray over your children before they go to school. Ask God to protect them, guide them, and give them wisdom, but don't stop there. Declare favor over them: "Father, thank You that my children have favor with their teachers, favor with other students, favor that is causing them to stand out, and favor that makes them excel." You are not only setting the course for their day, but you are declaring God's favor over their entire life.

If you've never experienced God's favor, if your life has been a series of bad breaks, know this: you can increase in favor. Luke 2:52 says, *Jesus increased in wisdom and in stature and in favor with God and man* (ESV). The way to increase in favor is by beginning to declare it. Every day, you need to declare His favor: "I have the favor of God. I have favor in my finances, favor in my relationships, and favor in my health." That's not just being positive — that's releasing your faith for the favor of God.

Today I choose to declare favor. Father, thank You that Your favor is continually on me.

TODAY I CHOOSE

To Walk by Faith

For we walk by faith, not by sight.
2 Corinthians 5:7 (NKJV)

When Moses led two million Israelites out of slavery into the desert, headed toward the Promised Land, I can imagine the people asking Moses, "Where are we going to camp? What are we going to eat? How will we find water? When will we get there?" I can imagine Moses's answer to every question: "I don't know." "I don't know where we are going to camp. I don't know what we are going to eat. I don't know how we will find water. I don't know when we will get there. All I know is, we are going to walk by faith."

Moses trusted God. He didn't have to understand how everything was going to work out. He didn't have to have all the details. He knew that God had a plan, and he was determined to trust Him one step at a time.

One reason God didn't answer all the people's questions upfront is that He knew they would have turned right back around and returned to slavery if they knew how long and hard the road ahead was going to be. Another reason is that if they knew how everything was going to work out, it wouldn't take faith. Faith is trusting what we can't see, not believing what we've already seen.

I'm the type of person who likes to know. I like to have a plan. I'm always trying to figure things out ahead of time. I used to get stressed when I didn't know, when I couldn't see a way, when there was no plan. But God has given me lots of opportunities to learn and grow in this area. Now I see that there are some things He doesn't want us to know ahead of time. There are times when He wants us to say, "I don't know, but I trust God."

God wants our faith to grow, and the only way that can happen is by learning to let go of needing to have all the answers. It is in those moments that you learn to walk by faith, not by sight.

Today I choose to walk by faith.
I don't have to have all the answers,
because I trust the One who does.

TODAY I CHOOSE

To Stop Running

And the Angel of the Lord appeared to him and said to him, The Lord is with you, you mighty man of [fearless] courage.
Judges 6:12 (AMPC)

When the angel called Gideon *a mighty man of [fearless] courage,* Gideon was hiding in a winepress. The Israelites had been oppressed by the Midianites, but God was ready to change all that, and He wanted Gideon to be the one to lead them out of their captivity. But Gideon said, *"How can I rescue Israel? My clan is the weakest in the whole tribe of Manasseh, and I am the least in my entire family!"* (Judges 6:15, NLT). Gideon was saying, "I'm not qualified." He wanted to run from his destiny because of fear and insecurity. But God reassured him, *"I will be with you"* (v. 16, NLT).

Some people spend their whole life running — running from the call of God on their life, from dealing with their temper, from forgiving that person, from writing that book, from ending that relationship, from taking care of their health. God is saying what He said to Gideon: "Stop running. I will be with you." *"Go with the strength you have. . . . I am sending you!"* (v. 14, NLT).

Stop sweeping things under the rug, ignoring issues and thinking they will just go away. God is giving you the strength, the grace, and the power to do what you couldn't do on your own. He is calling you a mighty man of fearless courage, a wonder woman of supernatural strength.

Judges 7 says that Gideon led the Israelites to victory over the Midianites and all their allies. He became the mighty man of fearless courage that God had declared him to be. He stopped running, faced his fears, confronted his insecurity, and became one of the heroes of our faith (Hebrews 11:32).

We all face times like Gideon where we have to make a decision: *Am I going to keep running, or am I going to stop?* If you want to move forward in life, you have to stop running.

Today I choose to stop running. I will face what I have been avoiding.

TODAY I CHOOSE

To Have a New Mindset

Don't copy the behavior and customs of this world, but let God transform you into a new person by changing the way you think. Then you will learn to know God's will for you, which is good and pleasing and perfect.
Romans 12:2 (NLT)

One day, when our son Jonathan was fourteen years old, we were out playing basketball. We played one-on-one, him against me, for many years. I could always beat him, but he kept getting bigger and better. This was the day that he would beat me for the first time. I played hard; I did my best, but he won.

What I remember most about that game was when he got around me and went up for a shot. I timed it perfectly. I came from behind, jumped with all my might, and blocked his shot. I swatted it over the bushes. It was epic.

A few days later, we were in the gym playing with some other guys. Jonathan said, "Dad, tell everyone what happened last week." I said, "It was great. You should have seen it. Jonathan went up for this shot, and I timed it perfectly. I blocked it. I swatted that ball into the bushes. It was epic." Jonathan said, "No, Dad. Tell them about how I beat you."

The funny thing is, that defeat wasn't on the front of my mind. That failure wasn't taking up the most space. My victory, my accomplishment, and my success were what stood out to me. And Jonathan didn't even remember the block. He just remembered winning.

If all you focus on is your losses, your flaws, your mistakes, and the times you didn't measure up, you won't become who God created you to be. You need a new mindset. You need a mindset that focuses on your victories, focuses on your successes, focuses on the times you were disciplined, the times you overcame temptation, and all the ways you have grown. When your mind is trained to focus on the victories, victory is what you will achieve.

Today I choose to have a new mindset. I will set my mind on the positive and step into the good, pleasing, and perfect will that God has for me.

TODAY I CHOOSE

To Abide

"I am the vine; you are the branches. Whoever abides in me and I in him, he it is that bears much fruit, for apart from me you can do nothing."
John 15:5 (ESV)

When Jesus was about to go to the cross, He told His disciples, "Abide in Me, and you will bear much fruit." He could have told them anything. He could have told them how to preach better, how to plant churches, how to work harder, be stronger, and perform miracles. But, as He was preparing to leave them, Jesus said, "This is how you are going to be successful, this is how to overcome challenges, this is how to fulfill your destiny: abide in Me."

The word *abide* in the original Greek means "to depend, to rely on, to relax." When Jesus told the disciples to abide in Him, He was telling them: "If you'll rely on Me, then you can relax. If you'll lean on Me, you won't have to strive to do it in your own strength. If you'll abide in Me, you'll bear much fruit." We think it would be the opposite: if you work harder, if you put in more hours and more effort, then you'll see the dream, then you'll get the promotion, then the problem will turn around. But Jesus says the opposite: "Don't stress yourself out; abide in Me. Don't try to do it in your own strength; let Me shoulder the load. Relax, and you will see God's favor."

Instead of depending on your own willpower, depend on God's power. Instead of stressing when challenges come, focus on His mercy and grace. God said, *"Apart from me you can do nothing."* When you focus on what you can do, you are limited. But when you abide in Him, He can take you twice as far in less time with less effort.

Jesus said, *"Come to me, all of you who are weary and carry heavy burdens, and I will give you rest"* (Matthew 11:28, NLT). If you are stressed, burnt out, and worried all the time, you aren't at rest. Start abiding in Him, and everything will get better.

Today I choose to abide. God, I am depending on You. When I keep connected to You, I bear much fruit.

TODAY I CHOOSE

To Surrender

"Father, if you are willing, take this cup from me; yet not my will, but yours be done."
Luke 22:42 (NIV)

The word *Gethsemane* means a "place of pressing." There was an olive grove in Jerusalem where workers would put olives in a press and, once squeezed, oil would come out. Before Jesus was crucified, He had to go through the garden of Gethsemane, the place of pressing. The pressure of what He was about to endure was so much, Scripture says He sweat great drops of blood (Luke 22:44). That's when He chose to surrender.

Surrendering is not the same as giving up. Giving up is saying, "God, it's too hard. I'm not doing it." That's not what Jesus said. Jesus said, *"Not my will, but yours be done"* (v. 42, NIV). He surrendered His will for God's will, knowing that God's ways are higher.

The real victory is in the surrender. Surrender says, "This betrayal is not going to make me bitter. This disappointment is not going to discourage me. This plan isn't fair, but I'm not going to get frustrated. I'm not giving up; I'm giving it to God. When pressed, the oil of gladness will come out, and I will declare, 'Not my will, but Yours be done.'"

How will you respond when the treatment isn't working? When your child is off course? When your dream is delayed? When the pressure comes? Will you blame, doubt, and want to give up? Or will you choose to surrender?

The apostle Paul said, *Our present sufferings are not worth comparing with the glory that will be revealed in us* (Romans 8:18, NIV). The squeezing, the pressing, the suffering — it may be present, but it isn't permanent. God will ask you to surrender your will to His will so that you can come through to the other side. On the other side of suffering, the scripture says you will come out established. You will come out stronger, better, with more favor and abundance than you could have ever known had you not been willing to surrender. On the other side of surrender, God will resurrect your hopes and dreams and take you into the fullness of your destiny.

Today I choose to surrender. Lord, not my will, but Yours be done.

TODAY I CHOOSE

To Take Care of Myself

With the crowd dispersed, he climbed the mountain so he could be by himself and pray. He stayed there alone, late into the night.
Matthew 14:23 (MSG)

If you spend all of your time making sure everyone else is a priority while neglecting yourself, you will wear yourself out. God doesn't want you to live depleted, drained, and running on empty. He wants you to take time to get refreshed, to be reenergized, to stay in balance and good health.

I love being productive, achieving, and feeling like I am accomplishing something, but I've learned that I'm not as creative when I don't take time for myself. For me, taking care of myself means laughing with my family, exercising, and playing basketball. When my wife, Victoria, needs to be refreshed, she goes shopping. She doesn't even need to buy anything; she just feels restored by walking around the mall. Everyone is different. Do what replenishes you. Go for a hike. Have coffee with a friend. Read a book. Go to the movies by yourself. Take a nap. Even if all you have is fifteen minutes, do what reenergizes you.

When Jesus was on the earth, everywhere He went someone always needed something from Him. Maybe you can relate. This kid needs to go to soccer and that kid needs to go to dance. Your spouse wants to tell you about their day, and dinner needs to be put in the oven. Your parents need driven to doctor's appointments, your boss needs the report by morning, and your best friend is going through yet another breakup. Christmas cards need mailed and someone needs to fill in at children's church every Sunday from now until eternity.

As the Son of God, Jesus had this incredible power, anointing, and wisdom, yet even He needed to be alone sometimes. Even He needed to get away from everyone needing something from Him. If Jesus needed it, why do you think you don't deserve it, too? It's not selfish to take time for you. When you're tired, you need rest. When you're drained, you need to be replenished. Work hard, make time for others, but don't forget about you.

Today I choose to take care of myself. I will take time today to do something just for me.

TODAY I CHOOSE

To Remain Calm

That You may give him power to keep himself calm in the days of adversity, until the [inevitable] pit of corruption is dug for the wicked.
Psalm 94:13 (AMPC)

Psalm 94 tells us that God has given us the power to remain calm when we face danger and difficulty. When we go around offended, upset, fearful, worried, and discouraged, it's dishonoring God. He has entrusted us with life. He could have chosen anyone to be here, but before time began, in His mercy, He handpicked you. He crowned you with favor. He is directing your steps. The way to honor Him is to go into each day with passion, being your best, pursuing what He put on your heart for that day, and remaining calm when life surprises you.

Because it will! Life will surprise you. People will push your buttons, and it will catch you off guard. You'll get a flat tire on the interstate; you weren't expecting it. Someone else will get the promotion that you were sure was yours. You'll be tempted to get upset, to explode, to complain. We don't get tempted to remain calm; that we have to do by

Would he settle for "better than it was," or would he ask for God's best?

It took vulnerability for the man to tell Jesus that He'd done okay, but He hadn't done all that He'd promised. Jesus honored that the man wanted the healing in full, not in part. And so Jesus touched him a second time and told the man to look again. This time, he was perfectly healed.

God knew what wouldn't work out in your life the first time. He knew the medical report wouldn't look great. He knew that relationship wasn't right for you. He knew you would get passed up for that promotion. Like He did with this man, God is waiting to see what you will do. Are you going to settle there? Are you going to be satisfied with "just okay"? Or are you going to ask God for a second touch? Are you going to be brave enough to look again?

Today I choose to look again.
Blurred vision is not my destiny.
God has a better plan.

TODAY I CHOOSE

To Serve

"And if you give even a cup of cold water to one of the least of my followers, you will surely be rewarded."
Matthew 10:42 (NLT)

Jesus made it clear to His followers: "If any of you wants to be great in the Kingdom, you have to serve others" (Matthew 20:26). He wasn't talking about serving once or on occasion. He was saying that, if you want to live a blessed life, you have to make serving others a lifestyle.

When serving is a lifestyle, you will understand that God has put people in your life on purpose so you can be a blessing to them, and you will look for ways to serve. Every day you can pray, "God, help me see the people You want me to serve today."

People who make serving a lifestyle are always helping a friend, volunteering in the community, encouraging a coworker, or taking care of a loved one. It's not something they force themselves to do — it is who they are, and who they are is truly happy because they aren't living to get but living to give.

The Scripture says that when you serve others, you are serving God. When you do it for them, you're doing it for

Him (Matthew 25:40). Every time you serve, God sees it. Every time you help someone else, every time you sacrifice, every time you go out of your way and pick up that friend, every morning you get up early to sing in the choir, every evening you stay late to clean up — God is keeping the record. Nothing goes unnoticed, and God says He will surely reward you. That word *surely* means "make no mistake, have no doubt, it will happen."

Now, people may not tell you thank you. You may not get the credit or the applause on earth, but when you serve others there is applause in Heaven. Almighty God sees your sacrifice. You're not doing it unto people; you're doing it unto God. He's the One that matters, and He is the One who will reward you in Heaven.

Today I choose to serve. I want my life to be of service, because whenever I do something for someone else, I am doing it for the Lord.

TODAY I CHOOSE

To Not Take Offense

Then Samuel asked, "Are these all the sons you have?" "There is still the youngest," Jesse replied. "But he's out in the fields watching the sheep and goats." "Send for him at once," Samuel said. "We will not sit down to eat until he arrives."
1 Samuel 16:11 (NLT)

When David was a teenager, his father, Jesse, didn't believe in him. One day, the prophet Samuel came to Jesse's house to anoint one of his sons as the next king of Israel, and Jesse didn't even call David in from the field. He thought David was too young, too small, nothing more than a shepherd boy. It was only after Samuel didn't choose any of the other sons that David was called in and then anointed as the next king.

Later, David took lunch to his brothers on the battlefield. His oldest brother belittled him in front of all the other soldiers. He asked David who he thought he was, why he was even on the battlefield, and why he wasn't taking care of the sheep. David could have been upset, offended, and angry, but David ignored him and walked away (1 Samuel 17:17–30).

The truth is, David's father was unfair, and his brothers were demeaning, but David had a destiny, and, in order to get there, he couldn't take offense. He couldn't let how they treated him prevent him from doing great things. He had to turn away from what they were saying and focus instead on what God was doing.

God knows what people have done to you, what they've said about you, how they've abandoned you and mistreated you. If you'll refuse to take offense, God will make it up to you. When you learn to turn away, you'll step in to new levels of freedom, joy, and victory.

When Samuel anointed David, his father was there to see it. When David defeated Goliath, the entire city cheered while his brothers stood back and wondered what happened. If you'll trust Him, God will take care of your enemies, and He may just promote you in their presence.

Today I choose not to take offense. I will not live bitter, angry, or offended. I am moving forward into my destiny.

TODAY I CHOOSE

Kindness

Your kindness will reward you,
but your cruelty will destroy you.
Proverbs 11:17 (NLT)

You can measure a person's spiritual maturity by how they treat people. Are you respectful to your spouse? Are you kind to your children? Are you courteous to other drivers on the freeway? Are you friendly to people at the store? Unfortunately, much of our society is not like this today. Too many people are rude, harsh, insensitive, and only worried about themselves. They bark orders instead of politely asking. They walk right by people without giving them the time of day. They blame others for going too slow, for being in the way, and for wasting their time. But 1 Corinthians 13:4–5 says, *Love is not . . . rude. It does not demand its own way. It is not irritable* (NLT). What ever happened to being understanding and going out of our way to show love?

Galatians 6:7 says, *A man reaps what he sows* (NIV). If you want people to be kind to you, you'll need to be kind to people. If you want others to show you mercy and grace when you make mistakes or unintentionally harm or annoy them, then you will have to show others mercy and grace.

Have you ever cut someone off in traffic? Remember that the next time someone cuts you off, and you'll be more likely to show mercy. Have you ever come home after a long day at work and been short with your spouse? Remember that the next time your spouse is short with you and show them some extra kindness. Have you ever made a mistake and had to ask for forgiveness? Remember that the next time someone wrongs you and be quick to forgive.

Jesus said, "*By this everyone will know that you are my disciples, if you love one another*" (John 13:35, NIV). He was saying there should be something different about Christians. Christians should be the kindest, most friendly, considerate, and loving people around. That's one of the best witnesses we could ever have.

Today I choose kindness.
I will look for people to be kind to,
and when others do something I
don't like, I will go out of my
way to be understanding.

TODAY I CHOOSE

To Come as I Am

When Jesus came by, he looked up at Zacchaeus and called him by name. "Zacchaeus!" he said. "Quick, come down! I must be a guest in your home today."
Luke 19:5 (NLT)

Zaccheaus was the chief tax collector in town, known for being corrupt. Yet, when he heard that Jesus was coming through town, he wanted to see Him. The problem was, the streets were filled with people, and Zaccheaus was short, at least a foot shorter than the average man at the time.

Romans 3:23 says, we *all . . . fall short of the glory of God* (NKJV). In some way, we're all short. Zaccheaus had wealth, but he got it by being dishonest. You can have a good marriage but still struggle with self-esteem or anger or jealousy. You can excel at work but not spend enough time with your kids or on your health.

We often work overtime trying to cover up our shortcomings, and that is exactly what Zacchaeus did. In order to mask his lack of height, he climbed a tree. Now he had an impressive position, the best view, so that later he could tell everyone how he had seen Jesus clearly from his vantage point.

Eventually, Jesus walked by the tree, and He stopped and looked up. *"Zacchaeus!"* He said, calling him by name. *"Quick, come down!"*

This was Zaccheaus's moment of truth. Up in the tree, he had the upper hand. He had the image of being impressive, and he could keep up appearances. But if he did what Jesus asked, if he came down, everyone would see his weaknesses, his shortcomings, and who he really was.

Jesus is asking you to come to Him as you are. You don't have to clean yourself up before you come to Him. You don't have to get your act together. You don't have to be free from jealousy or insecurity or have your bank account in balance. Jesus did not come to condemn you; He came to love you right where you are, because it is His love alone that will set you free.

Today I choose to come as I am,
with all my messes and mistakes.
Jesus, this is me.

TODAY I CHOOSE

Unconditional Trust

Trust in the LORD with all your heart and lean not on your own understanding; in all your ways submit to him, and he will make your paths straight.

Proverbs 3:5–6 (NIV)

It's easy to trust God when things are going our way, when we're getting good breaks, when our business is blessed, and when our children are happy. But what about when things aren't going our way? What about when our prayers aren't being answered, when our problems aren't turning around, and when we're not seeing favor? Too often, in those times, we get discouraged and think, *God, where are You? Did You forget about me? Why aren't You doing something?*

Conditional trust says, "God, if You'll meet my demands, if You'll answer my prayers my way, on my timetable, then I'll be happy. Then I'll believe in You. Then I'll praise You."

Unconditional trust says, "God, I don't like it. I'm uncomfortable, but I'm smart enough to realize that You're God and I'm not. You're on the throne. You control the universe. You said Your plans for me are for good. You said You would lead me down the best path for my life. Even though I don't understand it, God, I trust You."

We prayed just as hard for my father, when his health was declining, as we did for my mother when she received her cancer diagnosis. We quoted the same scriptures. We believed in faith. But my mother was healed here, and my father went to be with the Lord. If we had had conditional trust, we would have gotten bitter when my father died. But we chose to have unconditional trust. We chose to believe that God is a sovereign God. We chose to trust Him even when life didn't make sense. We chose to believe with all our hearts that He was still directing our steps.

You'll live a lot freer and a lot happier if you'll quit fighting what God is not changing. Trust Him when you don't understand. Trust Him when it feels like you're going the wrong way. Dare to trust Him, no matter what.

Today I choose unconditional trust. God loves me, and He has my best interest at heart.

TODAY I CHOOSE

To Keep the Faith

I have fought the good fight, I have finished the race, I have kept the faith.
2 Timothy 4:7 (NIV)

God has a great plan for your life, but that plan won't come without opposition. The enemy knows there is greatness in you. He can sense that you're a world-changer, a giant killer, and a history-maker. He brings difficulties into your life, bad breaks, and things that aren't fair because he's trying to get you discouraged. He wants you to live in doubt, lose your passion, and think God has forgotten about you. Don't fall into that trap. That's when you have to dig deep and decide that you are going to keep the faith.

Acts 9 tells how Saul encountered Jesus on the road to Damascus and went blind for three days. This experience led him to put his faith in Jesus, and his name was changed to Paul. You would think that his suffering would end there, now that he was devoted to Christ, but that was only the beginning of Paul's suffering. The Church refused to accept him at first. They didn't believe his conversion was real. Then Paul ended up in prison multiple times. He was beaten, shipwrecked, and had all these terrible things happen to him.

Yet, at the end of his life, he wrote to Timothy: *I have fought the good fight, I have finished the race, I have kept the faith.* Nothing that came against him stopped him from keeping his faith in God.

Whatever you are facing right now, whether it be in your relationships, your finances, or your health, you have to keep the faith. God is still on the throne, and He has a way out of this, even though you can't see it yet. He is still ordering your steps. Victory is coming, but in the meantime, you have to keep the faith. When you lose a loved one, keep the faith. When your job is eliminated, keep the faith. When sickness comes, keep the faith. Like Paul, God will give you the strength to fight to the finish. Just keep the faith!

Today I choose to keep the faith.
No matter what comes against me,
I trust that God is for me.
My hope is in Him!

TODAY I CHOOSE

To Break the Cycle

"The person who sins is the one who will die. The child will not be punished for the parent's sins, and the parent will not be punished for the child's sins. Righteous people will be rewarded for their own righteous behavior, and wicked people will be punished for their own wickedness."
Ezekiel 18:20 (NLT)

My father grew up in poverty. His family were farmers who lost everything during the Great Depression. He had to drop out of high school. All he had seen growing up was defeat, lack, and mediocrity. It looked like that was his future, too.

But at seventeen years old, my father gave his life to Christ, and he was the first in his family to do so. He felt God calling him to be a minister. He had no training, no money, no connections, and no family support, but my father told me that right then and there he determined that his children would never be raised in the poverty and defeat that he was raised in. He was determined to break the cycle.

When you look back in your family line, you will see things that have caused heartache and pain, things that have kept people from their potential. Just as you inherit your parents' DNA, which determines your eye color, how tall you'll be, and what kind of hair you'll have, you also inherit attitudes, habits, and behaviors from those who have gone before you. Research shows that depression, anger, addictions, and even low self-esteem can be passed down. Something may be in your bloodline, but it can stop with you. Like my father, you can choose to break the cycle.

You might think, *That's great, Joel, but everyone in my family is divorced. Everyone in my family struggles with their finances. Everyone in my family has addictions.* Let me tell you: You're not everyone. You're the exception. The favor of God is upon you. You have more knowledge than they did. You have the anointing. God raised you up to be the difference maker. The cycle stops with you.

Today I choose to break the cycle. Everything negative that was passed on to me stops with me.

TODAY I CHOOSE

To Obey

"Do not add to or subtract from these commands
I am giving you. Just obey the commands of
the L*ORD your God that I am giving you."*
Deuteronomy 4:2 (NLT)

In the book of Deuteronomy, God gave Moses the Ten Commandments. When Moses shared them with the Israelite people, he said: *"Do not add to or subtract from these commands I am giving you. Just obey. . . .* " He was saying: "Don't debate it. Don't overanalyze it. Don't try to figure it out. Just do what God is asking you to do."

Through the Holy Spirit, God speaks His commands directly to our hearts. However, too often, we feel these impressions, we have this knowing on the inside, but we dismiss them. We feel God nudge us to be good to someone, but we think, *I'll do it later.* A door opens that we've been praying for, but we overanalyze it and think, *That couldn't be for me.* God is saying to us what He said to the Israelites: "Just obey." Don't talk yourself out of it. Don't come up with excuses. Just obey.

When a friend of mine was a new believer, he was sitting in church one Sunday when God impressed upon his heart to give a gift to a woman who was sitting nearby. He argued with himself the whole church service about it: *She'll think I'm crazy. I don't even know her. Does she even need it?* Eventually he opened his wallet and saw that all he had was a five-dollar bill. *This is embarrassing,* he thought. *God, do You really want me to give her five dollars?* After the service, he walked over to the woman and said, "This may sound strange, but I feel like God wants me to give you this five-dollar bill." The woman instantly started crying. She said, "I only had enough gas to get to church, and I've been praying all morning that God would somehow give me the gas money to get back home. You are the answer to my prayer."

God knows what He is doing. He can see things that we cannot see. Don't talk yourself out of it. Just obey!

Today I choose to obey. I will be attentive to God's voice and follow where He leads me.

TODAY I CHOOSE

To Be Comfortable Not Knowing

For now we see in a mirror dimly, but then face to face. Now I know in part; then I shall know fully, even as I have been fully known.
1 Corinthians 13:12 (ESV)

My sister, Lisa, was born with a birth injury. Doctors said she would never be able to walk. My parents were devastated. They didn't understand why this would happen. Despite being taught in seminary that the day of miracles was over, my father prayed and read his Bible. He read about how Jesus went around healing people and doing so much good. He realized, there wasn't a *day* of miracles — there is a *God* of miracles, and He is still alive! Daddy and Mother prayed over Lisa and asked God to heal her. Little by little, she got better, and today Lisa is perfectly healthy.

My father went back to his church with a new fire inside. He started sharing about the Lord our Healer who wants us to live in victory. He thought everyone would share in his passion, but many of them didn't. It didn't fit into their tradition. There was so much discord, my parents had to leave that church. They felt the sting of rejection. They'd poured their heart and soul into those people, never dreaming it would come to an end like this.

What they didn't understand then was that God was closing that door, pushing them out, so that He could move them to the next level of their destiny. If it hadn't been for Lisa's injury and the rejection of the church, my parents may never have started Lakewood. We can look back on those seasons now and understand, but at the time, it didn't make any sense.

When difficulties come, you won't be able to see in the moment what God is doing. Scripture says someday we will understand fully, but until then, you have to believe that God is up to something. He is up to something good, even when you can't see what He is doing or where He is taking you.

Today I choose to be comfortable not knowing. Someday I may look back and understand why, but for now, I choose to trust the One who knows all things.

TODAY I CHOOSE

To Recognize My Value

Since you are cherished and precious in my eyes, and because I love you dearly and want to honor you, I willingly give up nations in exchange for you—a man to save your life.
Isaiah 43:4 (TPT)

Isaiah 43 says that you are cherished, precious, loved, and worthy of sacrifice. Those are God's words about you. Those are His thoughts about you. It is very powerful when you can receive them and believe them, when you can accept that this is how God sees you.

Most people can't do that. They think they have to change for God to love them. They think they have to be different to even like themselves. They think if they were a better parent, had a different personality, weren't jealous, hadn't made that mistake — then they would have value. Satan, the accuser, will make sure to remind you of something that you're not doing right, some area where you're not up to par, some way that you failed, but Hebrews 12:2 tells us that those are distractions. Instead, we need to focus on Jesus, who knows everything about us — the good, the bad, the ugly — and still thought each one of us was worth dying for (Romans 5:8).

Paul said in Ephesians 6:14 to put on *the breastplate of God's approval* (TLB). Every morning when you get up, you should say, "Father, thank You that You approve of me. Thank You that You accept me. Thank You that You are pleased with me. Thank You that I have value and I am precious in Your sight." You have to put on that approval. It's not going to automatically happen. It's not going to put itself on. The breastplate covers the heart, and you need to — on purpose — get the truth of how God feels about you deep down in there.

Your destiny is too important, and your time is too valuable, to sit around thinking about everything wrong with you. That's taking your joy, your energy, your creativity. Start looking away from all that and put on God's approval. You are His masterpiece. He created you. You have value because you are chosen, forgiven, cherished, precious, and wholly, dearly loved!

Today I choose to recognize my value. I feel good about who I am. Thank You God for loving me.

TODAY I CHOOSE

To Let Go

"Take your son, your only son—yes, Isaac, whom you love so much—and go to the land of Moriah. Go and sacrifice him as a burnt offering on one of the mountains, which I will show you."
Genesis 22:2 (NLT)

Sometimes, we want things so badly we think we can't be happy unless they work out our way. But God may ask you to let go of what you think you want so that He can give you what you actually need. If it consumes you, it's all you think about, it's all you pray about, it's always on your mind — then it's time to let go. It's time to put it on the altar and make God first in your life.

Abraham waited twenty years after God told him that he would have a son until he held Isaac in his arms. He and his wife, Sarah, prayed, believed, and stood in faith. They finally saw the promise come to pass. Then a few years later, God asked Abraham to take Isaac up a mountain and sacrifice him. God was asking Abraham to lay his dream on the altar. Abraham was willing. He didn't understand it; it didn't seem fair, but he was obedient. Just when Abraham was about to follow through, God stepped in. He saw that Abraham trusted Him more than anything.

Like He did with Abraham, there are times when God will ask us to put our dreams on the altar. God wants to see that we don't have to have the house to be happy. We won't live bitter and sour if we never have the baby. We'll keep smiling, even if our health never improves. We will let go of our way and trust His way. We'll keep Him first.

Many times, like with Abraham, God will reward your faith and give you back what you were willing to sacrifice. When you choose to let go of your own plan and trust God no matter what, He'll not only give you the desires of your heart; He'll bless you beyond measure.

Today I choose to let go. I want God's plan for my life more than I want my own.

TODAY I CHOOSE

To Grow

When I was a child, I spoke as a child, I understood as a child, I thought as a child; but when I became a man, I put away childish things.
1 Corinthians 13:11 (NKJV)

Several times in his letters, the apostle Paul compares spiritual maturity to a child learning to eat solid food after only being able to consume milk for the first year. In 1 Corinthians 3, he calls the people *infants in Christ* (v. 1, NLT). He says, *I had to feed you with milk, not with solid food, because you weren't ready for anything stronger* (v. 2, NLT). Hebrews 5:14 says, *Solid food is for those who are mature* (NLT). We all start as spiritual infants. God is kind and patient with us in this stage, but He doesn't want us to stay there. He knows when we are capable of more, and in order to grow, we'll have to take initiative, step out on our own, and accept greater challenges.

When the Israelites were in slavery, God seemed to take care of everything. He sent plagues, parted the Red Sea, and drowned their enemies while the Israelites just stood back and watched. In the desert, this pattern continued. God brought them water out of a rock, gave them manna to eat, and defeated their enemies. But the closer the Israelites got to the Promised Land, the less God did for them.

With the Promised Land came greater levels of responsibility. As they got closer, the Israelites had to grow up. God expected them to begin to stand on their own two feet, to encourage themselves, to fight off fear. He wanted them to participate in their healing, their victories, their new way of living. He wanted them to *put away childish things*, to start eating solid food, to step into maturity.

Growth is uncomfortable. That's why we fight it. But God doesn't want you to stay where you are. He wants to take you to new levels. He wants to trust you with more responsibility. He wants you to go higher than you've been before. He wants you to have greater faith.

Today I choose to grow — to grow in faith, to grow in maturity, to grow in responsibility. I know that God created me for more.

TODAY I CHOOSE

To Speak Life

For she kept saying to herself, "If I could touch even his clothes, I know I will be healed."
Mark 5:28 (TPT)

In Mark 5, there was a woman who had been sick for twelve years. She had spent all her money trying to get well. She went to all the best doctors, but they made her worse instead of better. One day, she heard that Jesus was coming through town. Mark 5:28 says, *She kept saying to herself, "If I could touch even his clothes, I know I will be healed"* (TPT). The ESV says, *"I will be made well,"* and the KJV says, *I shall be whole.*

In the midst of her sickness, she was prophesying health. Over and over, she kept saying, "Healing is coming; breakthrough is coming; wholeness is coming; my life is being restored."

Despite the crowds, she made her way to Jesus. With every step she declared, "This is my time. Healing is mine." Finally, she was close enough to reach out and touch Jesus' robe, and instantly she was healed.

Whatever you are constantly saying, you are moving toward. If she had said, "It's hopeless; I'll never get well," she would have moved closer to the grave. Instead, she kept saying, "I know I will be healed," and she moved closer to Jesus, the Source of abundant life.

When you say, "I am blessed," you're moving toward blessing. When you say, "I have the favor of God," you're moving toward increase and promotion. When you say, "I'm excited about my future; something good is going to happen to me," you are moving toward new opportunities and divine connections. When you say, "I'm going to break this addiction; I'm not going to live bound by this alcohol, by this anger, or by this bad habit," you are moving toward freedom, breakthroughs, and victory. Pay attention to what you're saying, because your life is going in that direction.

Proverbs 18:21 says, *Death and life are in the power of the tongue* (NKJV). Speak life, and you will reap the benefits of those life-giving words.

Today I choose to speak life and to keep speaking life. Every day, God is moving me closer and closer to my destiny.

TODAY I CHOOSE

To Renew My Faith

Then, looking into Thomas' eyes, he said, "Put your finger here in the wounds of my hands. Here—put your hand into my wounded side and see for yourself. Thomas, don't give in to your doubts any longer, just believe!"
John 20:27 (TPT)

When the disciples heard that Jesus had risen from the grave and people had seen Him alive, everyone was excited — everyone, that is, except Thomas. Thomas said he needed to see Jesus with his own eyes to believe.

A week later, the disciples were in the upper room when Jesus came walking through the door. Just imagine the commotion: Jesus was alive and in the room! What's interesting is, Jesus didn't go over to Andrew and say, "Andrew, I made it!" He didn't walk over to Matthew and give him a fist bump, or even John, His favorite, for a big hug. Jesus bypassed all the people who had faith and went straight to the one person in the room who had doubt.

Jesus went right up to Thomas, looked him in the eyes and said, *"Put your finger here. . . . See for yourself. . . . Don't give in to your doubts any longer, just believe!"*

When we have doubts, like Thomas, we can think God wants nothing to do with us. But it's just the opposite. Sometimes God will bypass the people with faith to go to the one person that has doubt, because He wants to restore your faith and remind you that He still has a plan for your life.

God doesn't judge you by one mistake. Thomas doubted one time, and we call him Doubting Thomas. But do you know what God calls him? Believing Thomas, Forgiven Thomas, Redeemed Thomas, Restored Thomas, Amazing Thomas. In fact, Thomas is so amazing that he is credited as being the one who went on to bring the Good News to the entire nation of India.

You may have failed, but you are not a failure. You may have doubted, but God says your faith can be made new. When you know who and Whose you are, you will become everything God has created you to be.

Today I choose to renew my faith.
Lord I believe; help my unbelief.

TODAY I CHOOSE
To Fear No Evil

Even though I walk through the valley of the shadow of death, I will fear no evil, for you are with me; your rod and your staff, they comfort me.
Psalm 23:4 (ESV)

Victoria and I were riding four-wheelers in the mountains one time when we came around a corner and saw hundreds of sheep on the trail. We couldn't get by. I honked. I revved the engine. I got as close as I could and honked some more. The sheep weren't afraid; they weren't even phased. We had to turn around and go another way.

Jesus told His disciples in Matthew 10:16, "*I am sending you out as sheep among wolves*" (NLT). Sheep are some of the most defenseless animals. They can't run fast. They can't hide. They can't bite. They can't growl. They can't even get up if they fall on their back. And yet, sheep aren't afraid. They don't worry. They don't have a care in the world. They trust their shepherd completely for their protection.

David was a shepherd who had spent years taking care of his father's sheep, keeping an eye out for dangers and fighting off wild animals to protect the lambs. When he wrote Psalm 23, the reason David could say, "I will not fear these darkest valleys," wasn't because he was so strong and courageous that he never felt fear. The reason he could choose to *fear no evil* was because he knew, *The Lord is my shepherd* (v. 1, ESV). Just as he cared for his father's sheep, he knew the Most High God was watching over him.

When you are tempted to fear evil, sickness, accidents, failures, and attacks, remind yourself: "The Lord is my Shepherd and He is watching over me." The reason we get worried, uptight, and afraid is that we're trying to be the shepherd when, in fact, we're the sheep. We're trying to do what only God can do when He is telling us to *lie down in green pastures* (v. 2, ESV). "Just relax," He is saying, "I will keep you safe."

Today I choose to fear no evil.
I turn my fears over to God and
trust Him to watch over me.

TODAY I CHOOSE

To Go to God First

So David asked the LORD, "Should I go out to fight the Philistines? Will you hand them over to me?" The LORD replied to David, "Yes, go ahead. I will certainly hand them over to you."
2 Samuel 5:19 (NLT)

When the Philistines heard that David had been made king over Israel, they mobilized their forces and prepared to attack. David was no longer a young shepherd boy. He was a warrior. He had conquered many enemies and won hundreds of battles, and now he was king. But here is why David was a man after God's own heart. Second Samuel 5:19 says, *David inquired of the Lord, "Shall I go and attack the Philistines? Will you deliver them into my hands?"* (NIV).

Notice David's humility. He took time to inquire of the Lord. Before he went to battle, he went to God first.

David asked a very significant question, "God, will You hand this enemy over to me?" It seems like that would be a given. God had just put him in charge of the Israelites, His chosen people. Surely God wouldn't let him be defeated.

But the fact is, we're not supposed to fight every battle. David was smart enough to ask, "God, do You want me to go and fight?" He was saying, "God, I don't want to go if You're not going to go with me." He was showing his dependence on God. He recognized where his strength, his favor, and his ability came from.

If we would do like David and go to God first — before we get into conflict, before we make decisions — it would save us a lot of heartache and pain. What God orders He will pay for, but God is not obligated to bring victory to battles we're not supposed to be in.

A few months later, the Philistines came back to the same valley to attack David again. Verse 23 says, *Again David asked the* LORD *what to do* (NLT). David didn't just go to God first that one time. He went to God first again and again.

Today I choose to go to God first. Not just today, but every day, because I need God's wisdom and direction again and again.

TODAY I CHOOSE

To Heal

The Lord is close to the brokenhearted and saves those who are crushed in spirit.
Psalm 34:18 (NIV)

Years ago, a company had a large amount of toxic waste that needed to be discarded. No one knew what to do with it. They had never had to get rid of something this dangerous and this toxic. Eventually they decided to bury the toxic waste in huge metal containers. They went to great lengths to make sure the containers were solid, sealed, and buried deep. They thought they had resolved the issue, but forty years later, the containers started to leak. The soil became contaminated, and then it spread to the water. People had to move away, and the company had an even bigger mess on their hands than they started with.

The lesson is, there are some things you can't bury. You can't bury anger and think it's not going to affect you. You can't bury bitterness and not have it leak out. You can't bury rejection without it contaminating your dreams, your attitude, your vision, and even the people around you. You can't bury shame and reach the fullness of your destiny.

This company would have saved themselves a lot of trouble if they had disposed of that waste properly the first time. You will save yourself a lot of heartache if, instead of burying what hurts you, you choose to face it head on and heal. It won't be easy. It will still hurt. But not nearly as much as if you wait.

We've all faced disappointments and things that aren't fair. It is natural to want to bury our pain, but when we push it aside, when we bury it deep, it will eventually seep into every part of our lives. The good news is, even if you have buried what hurts you, it's not too late to do something about it. You don't have to live with that heartache contaminating everything you feel and do. You can let it go. You can give it to God. You can choose this day to heal from what hurts you so you can be free.

Today I choose to heal. I am no longer burying my feelings. I will face them. I will give them to God. I am free.

TODAY I CHOOSE

To Receive Abundantly

Mary responded, "I am the Lord's servant. May everything you have said about me come true." And then the angel left her.
Luke 1:38 (NLT)

When an angel appeared to a teenage girl named Mary and said she was going to have a baby without knowing a man, and that He would be the Messiah, you can imagine Mary's first thought: *That's impossible!* She could have laughed at the angel and walked off, but instead she asked, *"How can this happen?"* (v. 34, NLT). The angel responded, *"The Holy Spirit will come upon you, and the power of the Most High will overshadow you. So the baby to be born will be holy, and he will be called the Son of God"* (v. 35, NLT). That probably didn't answer all of Mary's questions, but despite any uncertainty she may have still had, she looked at the angel and said, *"May everything you have said about me come true"* (v. 38, NLT).

It had never been done before. It didn't make sense. There was no earthly way it could happen. Mary wasn't perfect, and yet she said, "Let it happen. I'm all in. I receive what You promised."

You are going to have these times like Mary did where God wants to give you more than you can imagine, more than seems possible, more than you deserve. He wants to give you the house, give you the baby, give you the business, give you the miracle. Dare to do like Mary and say, "God, let it happen. I receive the abundance. I receive the blessing. I receive everything You have promised me."

Don't go through life pushing away all the good things God has for you because you feel unworthy. Every day, receive what God says about you: "I'm loved. I'm valuable. I'm approved. I'm worthy. I'm favored. I am a masterpiece." Luke 12:32 says, *"It is your Father's good pleasure to give you the kingdom"* (ESV). It makes God happy to bless you abundantly. It pleases Him when you receive the gifts He is offering you: the answer to your prayers and the fulfillment of your dreams.

Today I choose to receive abundantly. God, let it happen just as You said.

TODAY I CHOOSE

To Protect My Peace

But we all, with unveiled face, beholding as in a mirror the glory of the Lord, are being transformed into the same image from glory to glory, just as by the Spirit of the Lord.
2 Corinthians 3:18 (NKJV)

Too many people go around feeling wrong on the inside. They don't really like who they are. There is a recording of all the things wrong with them that keeps playing in their mind: *You're impatient; you lost your temper yesterday; you blew your diet; you're still struggling with that addiction.*

The truth is, when you focus on your faults and weaknesses, and you are constantly critical toward yourself, you will never be happy. You will never have joy. You will never have peace. But you're not supposed to go through life feeling badly about yourself. The way to protect your peace is to recognize that you're not a finished product. God is still working on you.

Scripture says God changes us *from glory to glory* (2 Corinthians 3:18, NKJV). You have to learn to enjoy the glory that you're in right now. You may have a long way to go, but look how far you've come. The Amplified version of 2 Corinthians 3:18 says you *are progressively being transformed*. You are making progress. You are better than you used to be — stronger, more faithful, less angry, more generous. We all have weaknesses and areas we know we need to do better in, but being down on yourself doesn't help you improve. All it does is steal your peace.

Jeremiah 18 says that God is the Potter and we are the clay. When you're on that potter's wheel, you're the easiest to work with when you're at peace with yourself. If you're uptight, angry on the inside, disappointed at where you are, it only slows down the process. God has to keep spinning and spinning. The right attitude is, "I may have some things wrong with me, but I'm at peace. I know I'm on the way. I know I'm in the process. God is going to finish what He started."

Today I choose to protect my peace. I accept that I am a work in progress. God is changing me from glory to glory.

TODAY I CHOOSE

To Listen to God's Voice

Anyone with ears to hear should listen and understand.
Revelation 13:9 (NLT)

The Holy Spirit is in each one of us to lead us and to guide us, and He speaks to us through a still, small voice. Having *ears to hear* isn't referring to our physical ears or an audible voice; it means hearing the Holy Spirit in your spirit, in your "inner ear" of knowing and understanding. And if you are obedient to what God's voice is telling you, then you will hear His voice more often and more clearly each time.

We know God says things like, *"Go into all the world and preach the Good News"* (Mark 16:15, NLT), but He also says: "Slow down on the freeway; quit eating so many sweets; forgive your coworker; be good to your neighbor." Pay attention to the practical things. The more you pass these tests, the more God can trust you and the more of His favor He'll release in your life.

One way you know it is God speaking to you is that you hear it again and again. When you're not even thinking about that thing, God will nudge you, He'll prompt you, He'll whisper in your inner ear what He wants you to do. Another way is that He will tell you things that you couldn't know any other way except through Him. Psalm 25:14 says, *The secret of the Lord is with those who fear Him* (NKJV). When you honor God, He'll tell you His secrets — He'll give you insight that you wouldn't have known otherwise. A third way you know it is God's voice is through the "I knows."

Have you ever said, "I know I need to eat healthier; I know I need to visit my parents; I know I need to be more disciplined in my spending; I know I need to call her; I know I need to tithe"? Here's a key: the "I knows" are God talking to you. "I know I need to forgive" is not just you deciding to forgive. That's God saying, "Do it!" Don't discount God's voice. Don't push it down. His voice is going to lead you down the best path for you.

Today I choose to listen to God's voice. I have ears to hear and believe He wants to speak to me.

TODAY I CHOOSE

To Focus on God's Promises

Let us hold unswervingly to the hope we profess, for he who promised is faithful.
Hebrews 10:23 (NIV)

Paul was a prisoner on a boat headed to Rome when an angel told him that he was going to stand before Caesar. That was a promise from God. But on the journey, they encountered a huge storm. For fourteen days, they didn't see the sun or the stars. The waves were so big, and the winds were so high, the men started throwing cargo overboard to keep the boat from sinking. The crew was so depressed they quit eating. The Scripture says, *All hope was gone* (Acts 27:20, NLT).

Paul could have been depressed too. He could have been angry that the men had set sail when he warned them it wouldn't be safe. He could have been afraid for his life. He could have given up hope. But Paul was none of those things. Paul was at peace because he was focused on God's promises. He focused on the words spoken by the angel, that he would see Caesar, because he knew God would keep His promise.

Because he had peace, Paul was able to encourage the crew. He told them, "Don't worry. We're all going to make it to shore. Not one life will be lost." The next thing you know, they were shipwrecked. All 276 passengers were in the water. Again, Paul could have doubted, could have panicked, could have given up. But again, Paul clung to God's promises, and everyone made it safely to shore.

Once on shore, Paul began to gather firewood when he was bit by a poisonous snake. Reading this, you are probably thinking, *Come on; can't this guy catch a break!* But Paul just shook off the snake and went about his business, keeping his focus on God's promises.

Storms in life will come. Shipwrecks and snake bites may threaten your peace. But when you focus on God's promises, you'll have a reason to keep hoping, keeping trusting, and keep believing, because God always keeps His promises.

Today I choose to focus on God's promises. He who promised is faithful!

TODAY I CHOOSE

To Make the Most of Every Opportunity

Live wisely among those who are not believers,
and make the most of every opportunity.
Colossians 4:5 (NLT)

Victoria and I had been married for a couple of years when we traveled to India with my father. On the way home, we stopped in Paris for a few days. We were so excited. It was our first time in Paris together. We couldn't wait to explore this romantic city.

Before we left home, we put an offer in for a house that we really wanted. It had a nice yard with big trees, and the house was light and open — everything we'd been praying for. Once we arrived in Paris, the first thing we did was call our realtor and ask if she'd heard anything from the sellers. She said, "Nothing." The next morning, we called again. "Any news?" "Still nothing."

During the day, we went sightseeing in Paris, but the whole time we were talking about that house. We were believing we were going to get it. We were decorating it in our minds. We were in Paris, but we weren't really there. We could have been making the most of that moment, enjoying the sights, taking in the beautiful city, and being romantic, but we were so focused on what we wanted back home that we missed what we had right in front of us. We weren't making the most of the opportunity God had given us.

If I could go back, I would say, "Joel, enjoy where you are. Make the most of this moment. At the right time, doors will open. Opportunity will come. But right now, enjoy your wife in this romantic city."

As soon as we arrived home, the agent called and said they'd sold the house to someone else. We had wasted our entire trip dreaming about a house that wasn't even ours.

Make the most of every opportunity. Don't miss your children, your spouse, or your friends. Live in such a way that nonbelievers want what you have — peace, joy, and contentment right where you are. Don't regret what you missed; appreciate what you've got.

Today I choose to make the most of every opportunity. I will live this day with purpose, intention, and gratitude for all that God has given me.

TODAY I CHOOSE

A New Attitude

Even though the fig trees have no blossoms, and there are no grapes on the vines; even though the olive crop fails, and the fields lie empty and barren; even though the flocks die in the fields, and the cattle barns are empty, yet I will rejoice in the Lord! I will be joyful in the God of my salvation!

Habakkuk 3:17–18 (NLT)

My sister Lisa went through a very difficult time. After a few months of marriage, her spouse said he didn't want to be married anymore. She was so devastated. She felt depressed; she felt shame; she felt hopeless.

After a few months, a friend of my father's called Lisa. He was a well-known minister. He said, "Lisa, I know you're hurting. I know it's not fair, but this is not the end of your story. The enemy is trying to keep you from your destiny. You have to rise up. Nobody can do this for you. You have to put on a new attitude and start moving forward. If you'll do this, God will take those scars and turn them into stars for His glory."

That was a turning point. Lisa didn't feel any different. She still felt discouraged, but she started ruling over those feelings. She chose a new attitude, and she started smiling by faith. When you smile, it not only sends a message to your body that everything's okay, but you're sending a message to the enemy that he does not have the final say.

Lisa was like Habakkuk, who saw barren fields but decided to rejoice anyway. Though the relationship didn't work out, though life threw her a curve, Lisa said, "Yet will I rejoice, yet will I believe, yet will I move forward, yet will I be joyful!" I like how the Message translation says it: *I'm turning cartwheels of joy to my Savior God* (Habakkuk 3:18, MSG).

The enemy wouldn't be fighting you if there wasn't something awesome in your future. Don't let a negative attitude keep you from your greatness. Choose a new attitude and start smiling by faith!

Today I choose a new attitude. What the enemy meant for evil, God can turn around and use for my good. Yet will I rejoice in God my Savior!

TODAY I CHOOSE

To Encourage

So encourage each other and build each other up, just as you are already doing.
1 Thessalonians 5:11 (NLT)

My mother had polio when she was a child. She had to wear braces on her legs, which led to one of them being shorter than the other. This caused her to walk slowly and with a limp. For decades, she was self-conscious about her legs and how she walked. When she was in her thirties, my father invited a minister friend to come speak at the church. The man was always very encouraging and uplifting. One afternoon, he and my father were walking behind my mother. The man leaned over to my father and said, "Just look at Dodie. She walks like a princess." That encouragement got down on the inside of her, and it changed her whole attitude. My mother no longer tried to hide how she walked. From that day forward and for the rest of her life, she walked like she knew she was royalty.

One compliment, one bit of encouragement, can have an impact for a lifetime. That's why it is so important that we encourage one another and build each other up. Everyone needs encouragement. Everyone needs someone cheering for them. Everyone needs to know that someone sees their value, that someone believes in them, that someone sees the best in them when the world is so often pointing out the worst.

The truth is, it's easy to see what people do wrong, but it's worth focusing on the things they do right. Words of encouragement can change the entire atmosphere in your household. If you want your house to be happy and full of life, speak encouraging words. You may even find that the things you wish your spouse would do will start getting done if you focus on building them up rather than tearing them down. When we use our words to encourage, it helps others become all they were created to be.

Look for who you can encourage today. If you'll do this, I believe and declare: not only are you going to help other people rise higher, but God is going to cause you to rise higher too.

Today I choose to encourage others and to look for ways to build people up.

TODAY I CHOOSE

To Turn Down the Noise

"You keep him in perfect peace whose mind is stayed on you, because he trusts in you."
Isaiah 26:3 (ESV)

A friend of mine is very upbeat and positive, but several years ago, I could tell he was changing. He became more serious, even distraught. He told me later that he had become so concerned about our country that he was consumed by watching the news, responding on social media, and debating with people he disagreed with. It had started to affect his sleep. He began having digestive problems. His relationships were strained. All the divisiveness, bitterness, worry, and negativity had begun to poison him on the inside. He finally got so frustrated he quit watching the news. Within a few weeks, he started sleeping soundly again. His anxiety went away. Today, he's back to his normal self, happy and fun to be around. If you let noise clutter your mind — negative news, worry, drama, gossip, fear, and divisiveness — it will steal your peace, and it might steal your health as well.

We are living in the noisiest time in history. There has never been a time when our world has been more divisive, had more distractions, and had so much competing for our attention. There is social media and twenty-four-hour news. Our cell phones make sure that we can be reached when we're driving, sleeping, and using the bathroom. We are never without the ability to be reached or informed. Many people are suffering from information overload. They are taking in so much news and so many opinions and theories that they have no peace.

Since the noise has been turned up, we have to become experts at turning it down. You have the volume control. You get to choose what you look at, how long you look at it, and what you allow in your mind. God wants to speak to you, but you'll never hear His "still, small voice" (1 Kings 19:12) if you are taking in too much noise. Guard your time. Don't waste it on drama with people who steal your peace or on guilt, worry, or negative chatter. Turn down the noise and tune in to Him.

Today I choose to turn down the noise. I have peace; my thoughts are on God.

TODAY I CHOOSE

To Let God Use Me

I replied, "The God of heaven will help us succeed. We, his servants, will start rebuilding this wall. But you have no share, legal right, or historic claim in Jerusalem."
Nehemiah 2:20 (NLT)

God put a dream in Nehemiah's heart to rebuild the walls around Jerusalem. They had been torn down, and now the people there were unprotected. The problem was, Nehemiah didn't live anywhere close to Jerusalem, and he didn't have the money or supplies to make it happen. Nehemiah could have let that dream die. He could have told God to find someone else — someone who had connections, someone who had influence, someone who lived closer. But Nehemiah chose to let God use him. Nehemiah chose to believe that if God had put the dream in his heart, God had also lined up everything he needed to succeed.

Nehemiah was working in the king's kitchen at the time, so he boldly went to the king and asked for permission to go to Jerusalem to work on the project. The king said yes.

Nehemiah told the king he would need protection and asked if he would write a letter to the leaders of the cities on the way to Jerusalem requesting safe passage. The king agreed. Nehemiah told the king he needed materials and asked him to tell the people who owned the lumber mills to give him what he needed. Nehemiah 2:8 says, *And because the gracious hand of my God was on me, the king granted my requests* (NIV).

When you choose to let God use you, His favor will be upon you, and you will be able to accomplish infinitely more than you could ever accomplish on your own. Nehemiah completed the rebuilding of the wall in just fifty-two days, because when you let God use you, you're on His timeline. He can accelerate things so that promotion will come faster, healing will come quicker, and your dreams will be accomplished much sooner than you anticipated.

When God puts a dream in your heart, do like Nehemiah. Choose to let God use you, and watch Him do the rest.

Today I choose to let God use me.
Nothing is impossible with God!

TODAY I CHOOSE

To Forgive Myself

Therefore, there is now no condemnation
for those who are in Christ Jesus.
Romans 8:1 (NIV)

God loves to use people who have made mistakes. Abraham had a baby out of wedlock, but God still made him the father of many nations. Jonah ran away from his calling, but God had him swallowed up by a big fish and gave him another chance. David took another man's wife and had her husband killed, but God still chose David for the lineage of Jesus. God doesn't disqualify us when we make mistakes, but we can make the mistake of disqualifying ourselves.

In Exodus 32, when Moses went up the mountain to receive the Ten Commandments from God, he left his brother Aaron in charge. Moses was gone so long the people got restless. They told Aaron they needed a god to worship. Aaron knew they were only supposed to worship the one true God — the same God who had spoken through Moses to tell Pharaoh to let the people go. Aaron had seen God deliver them from slavery and part the Red Sea. But he told the people to bring him their gold, and he melted it down into a golden calf that they could worship. When Moses came down the mountain, he saw Aaron dancing with the people, celebrating and worshipping that idol.

Did God tell Moses to wash his hands of Aaron? Did God say, "Aaron messed up; I can't use him anymore"? Not even close. God didn't write him off; God promoted him. God chose Aaron to be the first high priest.

Don't judge yourself based off of one mistake, one time when you gave in to temptation, or one season that you compromised. That didn't stop your destiny. The only way it will hold you back is if you live guilty and condemned. God has forgiven you for that, but you have to forgive yourself. He has given you His mercy, but you have to have mercy on yourself. There is nothing that you can do that God cannot forgive. He has already died for that. It's time that you choose to forgive yourself.

Today I choose to forgive myself. God has forgiven me, and if He can forgive me, then I can forgive myself.

TODAY I CHOOSE

Hope

Why, my soul, are you downcast? Why so disturbed within me? Put your hope in God, for I will yet praise him, my Savior and my God.
Psalm 42:5 (NIV)

In the days of King David, a king faced many trials: enemies waging war, men vying for the crown, social and economic challenges, not to mention the difficulty of having to try to please multiple wives.

David struggled with all of these, but the greatest battle, he discovered, was often in his own mind. David had doubts and fears, and he even struggled with depression. During one of those bouts, he spoke to himself and said: *So then, my soul, why would you be depressed? Why would you sink into despair? Just keep hoping and waiting on God, your Savior. For no matter what, I will still sing with praise, for you are my saving grace!* (Psalm 42:5, TPT).

In other words, he was saying to himself: "David, get your hopes up! Start dreaming again. Start believing again. Praise God no matter what. He is your saving grace." David started speaking hope, life, and victory to himself, and his spirits rose. Things began to turn around.

David said in Psalm 40, *He lifted me out of the pit of despair, out of the mud and the mire. He set my feet on solid ground and steadied me as I walked along* (v. 2, NLT). When you hope in God, He'll lift you up. And when your hopes are up, your feet and the ground beneath them will be steady. You won't feel like the rug is about to be pulled out from under you. You'll trust that what the enemy meant for evil God will turn around for good. You'll know that what the devil took from you, God will restore tenfold. You'll believe that your best days are yet to come.

You may have had some disappointments, setbacks, and unfair situations that you had no control over, but I'm telling you today to choose hope. When you choose hope, it not only keeps you strong and full of faith, but it opens the door for God to turn things around.

Today I choose hope. The Lord is my Healer, my Redeemer, my Protector, my Provider, my Savior, and my God.

TODAY I CHOOSE

To Not Settle

God will lavish you with good things. . . . God will throw open the doors of his sky vaults and pour rain on your land on schedule and bless the work you take in hand. You will lend to many nations but you yourself won't have to take out a loan. God will make you the head, not the tail; you'll always be the top dog, never the underdog, as you obediently listen to and diligently keep the commands of God, your God, that I am commanding you today.

Deuteronomy 28:11–13 (MSG)

In the story of the Prodigal Son, a young man went away and squandered his entire inheritance until he had nothing left. He returned home, and his father was so grateful to see him that he said, "*Bring the fattened calf and kill it. Let's have a feast and celebrate*" (Luke 15:23, NIV). The older brother, who had stayed home, was very upset. He said, "Dad, I've been here this whole time, and you've never even given me a skinny goat to share with my friends." His father responded, "*You are always with me, and everything I have is yours*" (v. 31, NLT).

God doesn't want you to settle for a skinny goat. He wants to give you the fattened calf. He wants to *lavish you with good things,* to pour out favor on your life. He wants you to start seeing yourself as *the top dog, never the under-dog*. He doesn't want you living on leftovers. He wants to bless everything you put your hand to. He wants to give you more than enough so that you can bless others with all that He has given you. Not because you deserve it. Not because you can earn it. But because He is a good, good Father. Don't settle for just some of God's blessings when He wants to lavish you with all good things.

Deuteronomy 1:11 says, *"May the Lord, the God of your ancestors, increase you a thousand times and bless you as he has promised!"* (NIV). That's my prayer for you — a thousand times more influence, a thousand times more resources, a thousand times more wisdom, a thousand times more because He has promised. Can you receive it?

Today I choose to not settle.
I want all that God has for me —
a thousand times more!

TODAY I CHOOSE

Fresh Manna

When the Israelites saw it, they said one to another, Manna [What is it?]. For they did not know what it was. And Moses said to them, This is the bread which the Lord has given you to eat.
Exodus 16:15 (AMPC)

When the Israelites were in the desert headed toward the Promised Land, God gave them fresh manna each morning to eat. This *"bread from heaven"* (Exodus 16:4, ESV) would only last for one day. Every morning, God told them, they would have to go out and get a fresh supply.

God tested them in this, and many failed. They thought, *I don't want to have to go out again tomorrow. I'm going to gather as much as I can today. Surely I can gather enough for a week! I'll save time and energy and get it all done at once.* But those who gathered more than they could eat in one day woke up to an unpleasant surprise: the leftover manna had spoiled. Exodus 16:20 says, *"It was full of maggots and had a terrible smell"* (NLT).

In the Lord's Prayer, Jesus taught us to pray: *"Give us this day our daily bread"* (Matthew 6:11, NKJV). He didn't say "weekly bread" or "monthly bread." He said "daily bread." Every morning you need to go to God for your daily bread, your daily wisdom, daily direction for your life. Not just on Sundays. Not even Sundays and Wednesdays is good enough. Because every day He wants you to come to Him for your daily bread.

The word *manna*, in Hebrew, is translated, "What is it?" When we go to God each day for that fresh manna, the right attitude is, "God, what is it that You want me to do today? What is it You want me to learn today? What is it You want me to speak today? What is Your manna for me?"

Our job isn't to give God orders, telling Him what to do and how to do it. Our role isn't to tell Him what we want and ask Him to bless it. Rather, we are to go to God and humbly ask: "God, what is it?"

Today I choose fresh manna.
I will seek God for what it is that
He wants for me today!

TODAY I CHOOSE

To Come Out Better

"I had only heard about you before, but now I have seen you with my own eyes."
Job 42:5 (NLT)

Scripture tells us that everything was going great for Job — he loved the Lord, and the Lord blessed him abundantly. But then Job went through a season of suffering. He lost his business, his children, and his health.

Job was distraught. He tore his robe in grief. He complained, he doubted, he feared, and he even felt self-pity. But then he got over himself. Job remembered that it is the Lord who gives, thus the Lord has the right to take away, and our responsibility as humans is to praise Him either way (Job 1:21).

Job declared, in the midst of his suffering, *"Though He slay me, yet will I trust Him"* (Job 13:15, NKJV). Job was saying, "Nothing is going to rob me of my faith. Not even death is going to keep me from hoping in the Lord!"

Keep trusting, and you will come out better on the other side. You'll come out with more faith. You'll come out with more joy. You'll come out with a testimony of all that God has done for you and how, even at your lowest, He never left your side.

God eventually healed Job and not only restored what he had lost, but God gave Job twice what he had before. But even before the double blessing, Job said to God, "*I had only heard about you before, but now I have seen you with my own eyes*" (Job 42:5, NLT). It's in those suffering seasons that we really get to know God. We read about His goodness and hear about it in church, but it's when we are desperate for Him that we fully experience His grace and mercy and love. It's when we are at our lowest, when God reaches down and comforts us, that we suddenly feel like we've seen Him with our own eyes for the very first time. That's why, after a tough season, you won't be the same as you were before that trial — you'll come out better!

Today I choose to come out better. This season will not steal my destiny; it will bring me even closer to God, who I can trust.

TODAY I CHOOSE

To Bless Myself

"Listen, I received a command to bless;
God has blessed, and I cannot reverse it!"
Numbers 23:20 (NLT)

In Numbers 23, the king of Moab hired Balaam, the prophet, to curse the Israelites. But when Balaam spoke, instead of cursing the Israelites, he blessed them. Balaam told the king, *"I will speak only the message that the LORD puts in my mouth"* (Numbers 23:12, NLT). A second time, the king asked Balaam to curse the Israelites, and a second time Balaam blessed them. This happened a third time, and a third time Balaam blessed them. The principle was this: man cannot curse what God has blessed.

God has put His blessing on you. You are set apart, favored, equipped, and empowered by the Creator of the universe. The enemy cannot curse you because you are blessed. But since the enemy can't curse you, he'll try to deceive you into cursing yourself.

Psalm 34 says, *Does anyone want to live a life that is long and prosperous? Then keep your tongue from speaking evil and your lips from telling lies!* (vv. 12–13, NLT). This isn't just an instruction not to lie to others or about others; it is also an instruction not to tell lies about yourself. Don't go around saying things that contradict what God says about you. When He breathed life into you, He put greatness on the inside. He destined you to leave your mark, to overcome that challenge, to outlast the opposition, and to take your family to a new level.

In order to see this good, long, prosperous, joyful, productive, and amazing life God has for you, you have to bless yourself. Blessing yourself simply means saying what God says about you. Say it out loud. Get in agreement with God. Each day say: "I am blessed. I am prosperous. I am redeemed, forgiven, talented, created, disciplined, focused, confident, secure, prepared, qualified, motivated, valuable, free, determined, equipped, empowered, anointed, accepted, and approved. Not average, not mediocre, I am a child of the Most High God."

Today I choose to bless myself. I am in agreement with God. I will only say what He says about me.

TODAY I CHOOSE

Freedom

When Jesus saw her, he called her forward and said to her, "Woman, you are set free from your infirmity."
Luke 13:12 (NIV)

In Luke 13, Jesus was in the synagogue teaching when He saw a woman who had been sick for eighteen years. She was bent over and unable to stand up. It was the Sabbath, when you weren't supposed to do any kind of work, so the religious leaders were standing nearby to see what Jesus would do. Jesus said to them, *"Should not this woman, a daughter of Abraham, whom Satan has kept bound for eighteen long years, be set free on the Sabbath day from what bound her?"* (v. 16, NIV). Jesus described the sickness as a chain. He said that she was bound. He said He didn't care what day it was. As a child of the Most High God, freedom was her inheritance. And so He touched her, and instantly she was healed.

Whatever has bound you, whatever has held you back, God is saying, "This is your time to be free." It is not your destiny to go through life with something limiting you. Galatians 5:1 says, *It is for freedom that Christ has set us free* (NIV). Another translation says, *Christ has truly set us free. Now make sure that you stay free* (NLT).

Freedom starts in your thinking, so get in agreement with God and begin to believe: This is a new day. Chains of debt are being broken. Chains of unworthiness are falling off. Chains of loneliness are being loosed. Chains of the past, you will see them no more.

Are there things that are holding you back? I encourage you to embrace this new perspective: "My chains are gone. I've been set free." Everything may not instantly change. You may have to walk it out. But the good news is, you're going to begin to experience freedom that you've never felt before. The fear will no longer hold you back. The depression will no longer steal your joy. The addiction will no longer control your life. The chain has been broken. You've been set free!

Today I choose freedom, freedom from the past and everything that has kept me bound. Jesus has not only set me free, but He wants me to stay free!

TODAY I CHOOSE

To Be My Authentic Self

So Jesus spoke to them: "You are masters at making yourselves look good in front of others, but God knows what's behind the appearance."
Luke 16:15 (MSG)

When Jesus saw Peter out fishing, He called him to be His first disciple, but Peter fell on his knees and said, *"Go away from me, Lord; I am a sinful man!"* (Luke 5:8, NIV). Peter was saying, "Lord, I have flaws. I'm hot-tempered and impatient. I use bad language. You don't want me. Choose someone else." Peter didn't try to cover up who he was. He didn't try to protect his image or pretend to be something he wasn't. He was honest, and later Jesus said to him, *"I tell you that you are Peter, and on this rock I will build my church, and the gates of Hades will not overcome it"* (Matthew 16:18, NIV).

Jesus could have gone to the temple and chosen the Pharisees, the religious leaders, to become His disciples. They looked the part. They knew all the laws. They prayed in public every day and taught in the synagogue. But Jesus said in Matthew 23:27, "*Woe to you, teachers of the law and Pharisees, you hypocrites! You are like whitewashed tombs, which look beautiful on the outside but on the inside are full of the bones of the dead and everything unclean*" (NIV). Jesus was saying, "You're all fake. You're pretenders. You wear masks, acting like you are better than everyone else. You may look good on the outside, but inside your hearts are wrong, and what God cares about is the heart."

The problem with the Pharisees wasn't that they had issues; the problem was that they pretended they didn't. That's why Jesus chose Peter, because He would rather work with someone who is open and honest than someone who tries to hide who they really are.

God is not looking for the fake you, the pretend you, the cover-it-up you. He's looking for the real you. Instead of hiding what you're struggling with, when you go to God and admit your dependence on Him, He will step in and strengthen you.

Today I choose to be my authentic self. God loves me and He can use me for His glory just as I am!

TODAY I CHOOSE

To Speak Victory

Let them shout for joy and be glad, who favor my righteous cause; and let them say continually, "Let the Lord *be magnified, who has pleasure in the prosperity of His servant."*
Psalm 35:27 (NKJV)

Psalm 35 says *let them say continually* that the Lord takes pleasure in seeing His people prosper. It doesn't say "Let them say it once"; it says *continually*. Over and over, God wants you to speak victory out of your mouth. Every day He wants you to declare that the Lord delights in your victories; He loves seeing you succeed.

Our words set the direction for our lives. If you want to know where you'll be five years from now, listen to what you're saying about yourself. Are you on course for a victorious life? Every day are you saying continually, "I am blessed. I am healthy. I am strong. I am surrounded by favor. Something good is going to happen to me today"? It's not enough to just think positive thoughts. We give life to our faith by speaking it out.

When you are going through a tough season, you can talk about the problem, or you can thank God that He is fighting your battles. You can complain about your circumstances, or you can thank God that He always causes you to triumph and that He'll bring you out better than you were before. Don't use your words to describe your situation; use your words to change your situation. Don't wait until you have the victory to declare that it is already yours. Invite success into your life by speaking victoriously!

Paul said in Ephesians 4:29, *Let everything you say be good and helpful, so that your words will be an encouragement to those who hear them* (NLT). One person who hears your words is you. Your words go out of your mouth and back into your own ears. What you say continually will take root in your spirit, so make sure what you are saying is good, helpful, and encouraging. You believe what you say about yourself more than what anyone else says. There is nothing more powerful than speaking victory over your own life!

Today I choose to speak victory.
I can do all things through Christ.

TODAY I CHOOSE

To Shine

"Arise, Jerusalem! Let your light shine for all to see. For the glory of the LORD *rises to shine on you."*
Isaiah 60:1 (NLT)

Isaiah 60 tells us to get up because it's time to shine. God's favor is on you. This isn't talking about someday in the future. Right now is your time to shine.

Esther was an orphan, Jewish and living in a strange land with no parents to raise her, when her uncle entered her into a beauty contest. Out of all the young women, she won and became queen of the Persian Empire. When the Israelites were on the verge of being annihilated, Esther went against protocol and presented herself to the king to ask him to spare her people. This was forbidden. She not only could have lost her position as queen, but she also could have lost her life. But Esther knew that the glory of the Lord was upon her. She knew that this was her time to shine. Her uncle even said to her, *"And who knows but that you have come to your royal position for such a time as this?"* (Esther 4:14, NIV).

God is looking for some Esthers, some men and women who will not shrink in fear, but who will arise because they know that He has created them for such a time as this, for this moment, for this great task.

Psalm 45:4 says, *Go forth to perform awe-inspiring deeds!* (NLT). You were not created to be average, to live a mediocre life, to hide in the shadows while others shine. You were made to take risks. You were made to rise higher. You were created in the image of God, created to do good works, created to perform awesome deeds.

God is saying to you, "If you'll arise, I'll cause you to shine. If you'll take steps of faith, I'll give you the wisdom, the creativity, the favor, and the abundance you need to succeed." There are awe-inspiring deeds right now prepared for you. You were made for such a time as this. Arise and shine!

Today I choose to shine. I will not bow down to fear. The glory of the Lord is shining on me!

TODAY I CHOOSE

To Believe What I Cannot See

"No longer shall your name be Abram (exalted father), but your name shall be Abraham (father of a multitude); for I will make you the father of many nations."
Genesis 17:5 (AMP)

Scripture tells us that we are to call things that are not as if they already were (Romans 4:17). Abraham is our example. God called him — by faith — *"the father of many nations"* long before Abraham had any children of his own. In other words, don't talk about the way you are; talk about the way you want to be. Say what God says. That's what faith is all about. In the world, you have to see it to believe it, but God says believe it and then you'll see it.

In order to get Abraham and Sarah to believe that they would have a child, God changed their names. In Genesis, it says that God changed Sarai to Sarah, which means "princess." He changed Abram to Abraham, which means "father of many nations." In other words, God changed the words they were hearing about themselves. Sarah was no longer a barren woman; she was a princess. Abraham was no longer without an heir; he was the father of many nations. You know the story. Eventually, at a very old age, Sarah gave birth to Abraham's son, Isaac. What God had spoken over them had come to be.

Words can do that. They can help us believe what we cannot see when we speak *those things which do not exist as though they did* (Romans 4:17, NKJV).

Words can also do the opposite. They can keep us in defeat when we say that we can't, when we say that it's not happening, when we say that we are not able. But God says that we are well able. He says that we are more than conquerors (Romans 8:37). He says, *"Let the weak say, 'I am strong'"* (Joel 3:10, NKJV), because He wants us to believe it before we see it. Instead of talking about the way things are, you can talk about the way you want them to be!

Today I choose to believe what I cannot see. I have faith in God, and I will call into existence those things which may not be yet — but soon will be!

TODAY I CHOOSE

To Love My Enemies

"You have heard that it was said, 'Love your neighbor and hate your enemy.' But I tell you, love your enemies and pray for those who persecute you."
Matthew 5:43–44 (NIV)

David went to the palace to work as one of King Saul's armor bearers. Saul was proud of David. He loved him like a son. Overtime, however, Saul became jealous of David. He could see God's favor on David's life. Instead of being happy for him, King Saul wanted to get rid of him. David had to spend months living on the run, hiding in caves, with King Saul and his men chasing after him and trying to kill him. More than once, David could have killed Saul, but he refused to harm God's anointed. Despite David being good to the king, Saul never changed his mind. He refused to have David back in the palace.

Several years later, Saul was killed in battle, and David was made king. Saul had proven to be David's biggest enemy, one that just wouldn't quit, and yet David loved him. When he heard that Saul had been killed, David wept (2 Samuel 1:11–12).

Years later, King David still had loving thoughts about Saul. He said to his staff, *"Is anyone in Saul's family still alive—anyone to whom I can show kindness . . . ?"* (2 Samuel 9:1, NLT). He wasn't bitter. He wanted to bless. He still wanted to be good to a man who wasn't good to him.

Jesus told us to love our enemies because He knew that — though difficult — loving and forgiving them would be better for us than holding on to unforgiveness, bitterness, anger, and hate. Loving your enemies is a choice; it doesn't come naturally; it's a decision you have to make. Jesus said, *"If you love only those who love you, what reward is there for that? . . . If you are kind only to your friends, how are you different from anyone else?"* (Matthew 5:46–47, NLT). God has called you to be different — not just to love your friends and those who love you but also to love your enemies.

Today I choose to love my enemies. Because God commanded it, I know it is for my benefit.

TODAY I CHOOSE

To Keep My Joy

Be filled with the Spirit, speaking to one another in psalms and hymns and spiritual songs, singing and making melody in your heart to the Lord, giving thanks always for all things to God the Father in the name of our Lord Jesus Christ.
Ephesians 5:18–20 (NKJV)

We have many types of birds near our house that love to sing early in the morning. They are so full of joy, as if they don't have a care in the world. They sing right outside our bedroom window and, many mornings, they sing so loudly they wake me up.

One morning, a storm hit when it was still dark. There was thunder and lightning, and the rain was coming down hard. I thought it was a good day to sleep in. About that time, I started hearing those birds right outside my window begin to sing. I couldn't believe it. They were singing right through the storm.

We need to take a lesson from those birds. When it storms, if we want to keep our joy, we have to keep singing. We have to keep being grateful. We have to keep making melody in our hearts.

Many times, in life, you won't be able to control your circumstances — what happens to you on the outside. But you can control what happens inside of you. That is where your joy comes from. You can choose to make melody in your heart and to keep a song of praise on your lips regardless of what's happening around you. You can choose to believe that God is fighting your battles for you. You can choose to believe that He is in control. You can choose to believe that He will make beauty for ashes and work all things together for your good. You can choose to be continually filled with the Holy Spirit through songs of praise and words of gratitude and, when you do so, you will keep your joy.

Today I choose to keep my joy.
I will keep a melody in my heart
regardless of my circumstances
because no matter what I face,
my God is greater!

TODAY I CHOOSE

Powerful Thinking

But Peter said, "I don't have any silver or gold for you. But I'll give you what I have. In the name of Jesus Christ the Nazarene, get up and walk!"
Acts 3:6 (NLT)

Acts 3 tells the story of a man who had been crippled since birth. Every morning, people would carry him to the gate of the temple so he could beg. When someone passed by, he would hold out his cup in hopes of a few coins. The cup was how he survived.

One day, Peter and John headed to the temple to pray. As they passed by the man, he held up his cup. Peter stopped, looked the man in the eye, and said, *"I don't have any silver or gold for you"* (Acts 3:6, NLT). I'm sure the man was disappointed, wondering why Peter had stopped if he wasn't going to bless him. Then Peter held out his hand.

In order to take Peter's hand, the man would have had to put down his cup. As soon as he did, Peter grabbed the man's hand, pulled him to his feet, and *the man's feet and ankles were instantly healed and strengthened* (v. 7, NLT).

It is significant that the man had to put down his cup before he could receive his miracle. He was hoping for a few coins, but God had a blessing so big that the cup couldn't contain it. In fact, the man would never have to use that cup again.

As long as you have a "cup mentality," you'll be sitting on the sidelines, thinking you are stuck, hoping someone will give you a break, hoping for just enough to get by. God is saying, "Get rid of your cup." God is telling you to choose powerful thinking, to believe that what He has for you is something you've never seen before.

Quit making excuses. Quit coming up with every reason why you can't be successful, can't get well, can't live free, can't get married, and can't go to new levels. That is limited thinking, and what God wants to do in your life can't fit inside that cup.

Today I choose powerful thinking. What God has planned for my life is greater than anything anyone has ever seen before!

TODAY I CHOOSE

To Agree with God

Abraham was first named "father" and then became a father because he dared to trust God to do what only God could do: raise the dead to life, with a word make something out of nothing. When everything was hopeless, Abraham believed anyway, deciding to live not on the basis of what he saw he couldn't do but on what God said he would do.
Romans 4:17–18 (MSG)

People will call you what you are *after* you become it, but God calls you what you are *before* you become it. In fact, God doesn't call you what you are; He calls you what you can become.

When you're sick and the medical report says you won't get well, God calls you healthy, whole, and strong. When the odds are against you, and you don't have the finances, the connections, or the education, God calls you successful, prosperous, out of debt, the head and not the tail. When you're struggling with an addiction and everybody in your family has had the same struggle, if you'll listen, you'll hear God saying, "You are free; this addiction is temporary; you're the difference-maker; the buck stops with you."

Don't make excuses. Don't come up with all the reasons why it's not going to happen. God will speak things over you that don't seem logical, but you don't have to figure it out; all you have to do is believe. Just get in agreement with God and you will become what He's called you to be.

There are promises that God has spoken over you, goals and dreams He placed in your heart. You didn't come up with them on your own. God put them there. Those *secret petitions of your heart* (Psalm 37:4, AMPC) are your destiny calling out to you; they are God telling you what you can become.

Get good at believing what God says about you. He is looking for someone who will agree with Him — someone who will rise up in faith like Abraham, who decided *to live not on the basis of what he saw he couldn't do but on what God said he would do* (Romans 4:18, MSG).

Today I choose to agree with God.
I will become who He says I am.

TODAY I CHOOSE

To Trust God's Timing

Yet God has made everything beautiful for its own time. He has planted eternity in the human heart, but even so, people cannot see the whole scope of God's work from beginning to end.
Ecclesiastes 3:11 (NLT)

In Mark 11, Jesus was returning to Jerusalem with His disciples when He said to two of them: *"Go into that village over there. As soon as you enter it, you will see a young donkey tied there that no one has ever ridden. Untie it and bring it here"* (v. 2, NLT). The disciples went to the village and found everything just as Jesus said. They untied the colt, brought it to Jesus, and He rode it into the city of Jerusalem on Palm Sunday.

Imagine this colt. Perhaps he had been tied up his whole life, wishing he could run, play, have fun, or at least carry someone or do some work like the other donkeys. Maybe he felt forgotten, disadvantaged, held back, wondering when he would come into his time. What the colt could not have known was that he was tied up for a divine purpose.

Hundreds of years before Jesus' birth, Zechariah prophesied: *Rejoice, O people of Zion! Shout in triumph, O people of Jerusalem! Look, your king is coming to you. He is righteous and victorious, yet he is humble, riding on a donkey—riding on a donkey's colt* (Zechariah 9:9, NLT).

This colt thought he was restricted, but really he was being reserved. God had set him apart, kept anyone from riding him, and tied him to that post so he would be in the right place at the right time for God to use him for a purpose greater than he ever imagined. Like that colt, God planned every detail of your life before you were formed in your mother's womb (Jeremiah 1:5), and God has something in store for you that is beyond your wildest imagination.

When God has you in a season of waiting, when doors are seemingly opening for everyone else but God is keeping you right where you are — trust His timing. He has set you apart for a higher purpose!

Today I choose to trust God's timing. He has ordered my life, and my time is in His hands.

TODAY I CHOOSE

To Enlarge My Vision

"Here's what you do," said Elisha. "Go up and down the street and borrow jugs and bowls from all your neighbors. And not just a few—all you can get."
2 Kings 4:3 (MSG)

In 2 Kings 4, there was a widow who discovered that her husband had died with a great deal of debt. The man to whom he owed the money was now on his way to collect. Since she couldn't pay him, he was coming to take her two sons as slaves.

The woman cried out to the prophet Elisha for help. He said, *"Tell me, what do you have in your house?"* She said, *"Nothing . . . except a small jar of olive oil"* (v. 2, NIV). Elisha told her to go to her neighbors and borrow as many empty containers as possible. He said specifically to *borrow not a few* (2 Kings 4:3, KJV).

As instructed, she went out and gathered empty containers. Elisha then told her to pour the little oil she had into one of the empty jugs. She filled the first container and discovered that she still had more oil. She filled the second container — still more oil. She filled another and another and another. Finally, when there were no more containers left, the oil stopped flowing. She then went out, sold the oil, and not only paid off her husband's debts but had plenty left over for her and her sons to live on.

Do you see that the woman determined how much oil she was going to have? The oil didn't run out until she was out of containers. That's why God told her to *borrow not a few.* If she had borrowed twice as many containers, she would have had twice as much oil. But if she'd thought just one or two containers would be enough, she would have gotten only one or two containers worth of oil.

God has an unlimited supply of love, grace, mercy, blessings, and favor that He wants to pour out in your life, but it's up to you how much you will receive. Don't let disappointments, delays, and mistakes limit your expectations. Stretch, believe for great things, and enlarge your vision. God is going to fill the containers you bring Him.

Today I choose to enlarge my vision. I will receive ALL that God has for me.

TODAY I CHOOSE

To Keep Praying

The rain continued to fall for forty days and forty nights.
Genesis 7:12 (NLT)

In Scripture, forty is a symbolic number used to describe a season of trials and adversity. After Noah built the ark, it rained for forty days. After the Israelites were rescued out of Egypt, they wandered in the desert for forty years. After Jesus was baptized, he was tempted for forty days. In life, we will have some of these forty-day experiences, seasons when the rains just won't quit. The medical report isn't improving. The bills keep piling up. The breakthrough isn't coming. Your spouse is lost in the wilderness and can't find their way to you.

When you are in a forty-day season, you'll be tempted to give up, tempted to doubt, tempted to think that things will never get better. That's when you need to keep praying! Keep praying — because your day forty-one is coming.

Scripture says that while Noah and his family were in the ark, it rained for forty days and forty nights. But on day forty-one, the rains stopped. Scripture says Goliath taunted the Israelites for forty days, paralyzing them with fear, but on day forty-one, David took him down with a sling and a stone. Scripture says Jesus was tempted in the desert for forty days by the enemy, but on day forty-one, the angels showed up and cared for Him.

You may be in a forty-day season right now, but your day forty-one is coming. Ezekiel 29:13 says, *At the end of the forty years . . .* (NLT). There is an end to this season. That job promotion will come through. That health concern will resolve itself. That spouse will finally get a GPS signal and will come knocking on your door. Day forty-one is when you see restoration, beauty for ashes, and God working all things together for your good. You're on the verge of receiving all that you've been praying for.

These forty days aren't for nothing. They are strengthening your faith, your prayers, and your ability to go through hard things. Don't listen to the lies that say it's never going to happen. God has set an end to your difficulty. Your day forty-one is coming!

Today I choose to keep praying. My breakthrough is right around the corner.

TODAY I CHOOSE

To Become New

Therefore, if anyone is in Christ, he is a new creation; old things have passed away; behold, all things have become new.
2 Corinthians 5:17 (NKJV)

When you have new software for your phone or computer, it requires a reboot. Rebooting can be inconvenient. You have to shut down your device, wait while everything updates, and then restart. But once the reboot is done, your device operates on a new level. It can do things it couldn't do before. It has better speed, more capability, and optimum performance. None of this would have been possible without the reboot.

It's the same with God. He didn't create you and say, "Okay you're done. You're all you're going to be." He's constantly upgrading our software — giving us new ideas, new abilities, and new perspectives. He's getting you prepared to do more, to go where you've never gone, and to accomplish dreams that you didn't think were possible. Scripture says, *Old things have passed away; behold, all things have become new* (2 Corinthians 5:17, NKJV).

When my computer has an update, it will say, "To receive this update, press yes." I could think, *My computer is working fine; I'm happy with it; I don't need the update,* and press "no." Or, if it is an inconvenient time, if I'm in the middle of something, I might say, "postpone" and "remind me later." I wonder how many of us are not updating to the new software that God is offering us. We're satisfied with the old, stuck in what was. We don't want to be inconvenienced; we don't want to have to get out of our comfort zone.

It's time to step into the new things God is doing. Press "yes" to that new attitude, that new way of seeing yourself, and that new talent, new opportunity, new vision. God wants to take you where you've never been, bring talent out that you didn't know you had, and give you wisdom, ideas, and creativity in greater ways.

Now, get in agreement with Him and receive it. Don't postpone it. The scripture says if *anyone* is in Christ, that person is a new creation — that person is you!

Today I choose to become new.
Out with the old, in with the new!

TODAY I CHOOSE

To Rely on God

"Behold, I am doing a new thing; now it springs forth, do you not perceive it? I will make a way in the wilderness and rivers in the desert."
Isaiah 43:19 (ESV)

When the Israelites wandered in the desert on their way to the Promised Land, they got thirsty. They needed water, but water was scarce. So, God told Moses to strike a rock. He did, and water flowed from it freely (Exodus 17:6). It was a miracle! The people got thirsty again, and this time God told Moses to speak to the rock. But Moses didn't listen. He thought, *I've seen this before. I don't need God's help. I know how to get water from the rock.* So he struck the rock twice, and water came out again, but the Lord rebuked him and actually delayed their entry to the Promised Land (Numbers 20:8–12).

God didn't want to do the miracle the same way a second time. Why not? Because God wants us to rely on Him, not some formula. God will do things differently so that we will have to come to Him every day with everything we face — even if we've faced it before. He will change the method on purpose so that we will have to rely on Him in order to succeed.

Have you ever heard someone say: "But we've always done it that way"? The world is moving forward, changing all the time. You can't afford to stay on autopilot, just coasting and doing things the same way you've always done them. You won't make it to the promised land God has for you. The truth is, God wants to do a new thing, a new way, with new ideas and new people to bring new talents out of you, to take you into the fullness of your destiny. But He's not going to let you do things on your own without Him. He'll change it up; He'll make all things new. You'll have to listen to His instruction and rely on Him.

Are you stuck, still striking the rock when God is telling you to speak to it? If you'll rely on Him and stay open to His ways, and listen to what He is saying *now*, then you will see water begin to flow in greater ways. He'll lead you further than you could ever go on your own.

Today I choose to rely on God. Faith isn't a formula; faith is daily reliance on Him.

TODAY I CHOOSE

To Stay Positive

"I think myself happy, King Agrippa, because today I shall answer for myself before you concerning all the things of which I am accused by the Jews."
Acts 26:2 (NKJV)

The apostle Paul went through a lot of bad breaks. In 2 Corinthians 11, he lists some of those difficulties: five times he was given thirty-nine lashes, three times he was beaten with rods, once he was stoned, and three times he was shipwrecked. We also know he was bitten by a poisonous snake, faced angry mobs, fought off bandits, survived flooded rivers, and was imprisoned countless times. He'd gone without food, proper clothing, and had many sleepless nights. He *faced death again and again* (2 Corinthians 11:23, NLT). Nobody, it seems, had more come against them than Paul.

After being in prison for two years, Paul was brought before King Agrippa for his trial. When he stood up to give his defense, the first thing he said was: "*I think myself happy*" (Acts 26:2, NKJV).

You would think Paul would have seen himself as a victim. You would think he would have considered himself unfortunate, bitter, angry, discouraged, even depressed. And if he'd been focusing on his difficulties, if he had been dwelling on his hurts, his rejections, and his fears, then he certainly would have thought himself miserable. But Paul chose to think himself happy. Paul chose to consider the cross rather than his own difficulties. Paul chose to believe God was still in charge. Paul chose to believe that something good would come out of every trial. Paul chose to stay positive.

You have no doubt gone through disappointments, challenges, and seasons when everything was coming against you and nothing felt fair. Don't dwell on those things. It is time to move on. You need to do like Paul and start thinking yourself happy.

We should feel a responsibility to live each day in faith — happy, joyful, and good-natured. Once this day is over, we can never get it back. We don't have time to waste another minute being negative, discouraged, focused on what didn't work out, and complaining over who did us wrong. Instead, see this day as a gift from God and choose to stay positive regardless of your circumstances.

Today I choose to stay positive.
I will not dwell on the negative.
Like Paul, I will stay positive
regardless of my circumstances.

TODAY I CHOOSE

To Reframe My Thinking

Everything is pure to those whose hearts are pure. But nothing is pure to those who are corrupt and unbelieving, because their minds and consciences are corrupted.
Titus 1:15 (NLT)

How you view your life will determine how you live. If you have a pure heart and a positive perspective, you will see your home, your spouse, your children, your job, and your life as blessings. But if you look at those exact same circumstances through a negative lens, you won't see blessings — you will see burdens.

For example, you can say, "I hate my job. I don't want to go to work. They don't pay me enough. My coworkers aren't good people. They don't treat me right. I'll never have the job I really want." Or you can say, "This job is a blessing. I am blessed that I get to go to work. Others wish they had this job. One day, I will have a job that pays more, but today I am grateful for the job that I have."

If you focus on the burden, you miss the blessing. But when you reframe your thinking, you can enjoy today and trust God to bless you tomorrow. God will bless you with more in the future when He knows He can trust you. As the Scripture says, *"Whoever can be trusted with very little can also be trusted with much, and whoever is dishonest with very little will also be dishonest with much"* (Luke 16:10, NIV).

Rather than complain about what your spouse doesn't do, thank them for what they are doing. Rather than complain about your children, thank God for trusting you to be their parent. Rather than complain about your church, thank God for the freedom to worship Him.

The enemy would love for you to miss out on God's blessings by wasting your years focusing on your burdens, but God wants you to enjoy the life He has given you. It's not complicated; it's just reframing your thinking, shifting your perspective from focusing on the burden to focusing on the blessing.

Today I choose to reframe my thinking. With God's help, I will shift my perspective from seeing what's wrong to seeing what's right.

TODAY I CHOOSE

To Be Present

"Give your entire attention to what God is doing right now, and don't get worked up about what may or may not happen tomorrow. God will help you deal with whatever hard things come up when the time comes."
Matthew 6:34 (MSG)

So often, our minds are either in the past, focused on what didn't work out, the mistakes we made, and who did us wrong — or in the future, thinking about our goals, worried about our finances, and wondering when answers will come. But we can't change the past no matter how much we think about it, and, as Matthew 6 attests, it's a waste of time to worry about the future when what you are worried about might not happen at all!

The problem with living in the past or living in the future is that you miss the present. David said in Psalm 118:24, *This is the day the Lord has made* (NLT). Today, this day, is a gift from God. Are you fully engaged, making the most of every moment, loving your family, and showing appreciation for all that God has given you today? Or is your mind still in yesterday or already looking to tomorrow?

When you are home with your family, be all there. Don't just go through the motions. Don't have conversations while also being on your phone. Give your kids, your spouse, and your parents your time. Connect. Listen. You won't always have your parents to talk to. Your kids will go from babies to teenagers to out of the house before you know it. Your marriage isn't going to thrive on yesterday. Grow together. Laugh together. Eat together. Show up for one another.

When life called the roll today, did you show up? Did you raise your hand and say, "Here. Present. Engaged. Ready to make the most of this day!" Once we live this day, we can't get it back. Don't waste it regretting yesterday. Don't lose it by worrying about tomorrow. Appreciate the beauty of this moment and the good things that are in your life right now while you still can.

Today I choose to be present. I will stay in the moment. I will connect with the people in my life. I will be all here.

TODAY I CHOOSE

To Pick Up the Mantle

He picked up the mantle of Elijah that fell off him, and went back and stood by the bank of the Jordan.
2 Kings 2:13 (AMP)

When Elijah went to Heaven, Elisha picked up his mantle. This wasn't just his coat; the mantle represented the favor, the authority, and the blessing of God. This was a critical moment. God was calling Elisha to greater things and giving him an opportunity to step up to a new level of his destiny. Elisha picked up that mantle and immediately the waters of the Jordan parted, and Elisha walked through on dry ground.

God is a progressive God. He wants every generation to increase, so He has these destiny moments where we are given the opportunity to pick up the mantle and carry it from one generation to the next. We can step into new levels of faith and favor. Often this happens when someone goes to be with the Lord. Their work here on earth is finished, but the purposes of God never stop. They finished their course, but they left the mantle for someone else to pick up.

My mother lived to be ninety-one years old. She carried lots of different mantles in her life — the mantle of faith, the mantle of prayer, the mantle of commitment, and the mantle of generosity. When she had her homegoing in 2025, God said, "Who is going to pick up these mantles?" It's not just for one; any of us can, all of us can.

God is calling all of us to greater things. He wants to know: Who is going to stand in the gap for that loved one who is off course? Who is going to cover your family with prayer? Who is going to believe for miracles in a greater way? Who is going to carry the mantle to live with greater commitment? Who is going to pick up the mantle of generosity, of being a blessing? God is calling us higher. He is saying there are greater things in store, but you have to pick up the mantle.

Today I choose to pick up the mantle. God, direct me to the mantles that You have chosen for me. I believe this is a destiny moment!

TODAY I CHOOSE

To Laugh

"God blesses you who are hungry now, for you will be satisfied. God blesses you who weep now, for in due time you will laugh."
Luke 6:21 (NLT)

We all go through seasons of struggle — seasons where we're working hard and not making progress, seasons of illness, seasons of loss, seasons of loneliness, seasons that we don't understand, and seasons that aren't fair. It is easy to think that the suffering, the struggle, and the weeping will never end, but Jesus said to those who weep: *"In due time you will laugh."* You will! Weeping is not how your story ends. The promise God makes us is not that we won't suffer, but that when we do suffer, it will only be for a season.

God sees what you are going through. Scripture says, *You've kept track of my every toss and turn through the sleepless nights, each tear entered in your ledger, each ache written in your book* (Psalm 56:8, MSG). You may have felt alone, but He's been right there with you, and He's not going to leave you brokenhearted.

First Peter 5:10 says, *After you have suffered a little while, he will restore, support, and strengthen you, and he will place you on a firm foundation* (NLT). You may be in a season of suffering, but it's not going to last your whole life. It's not going to linger for another twenty years. God says it will last a *little while*, but then look what He will do after that — God Himself will step in and restore you, support you, strengthen you, and place your feet on solid ground. He will pay you back for what was unfair. He will turn your mourning into dancing, your sorrow into joy, and your weeping into laughter. He will bring you out better. Don't believe those lies that you will never laugh again. Your time is coming. Joy is on the way. You will laugh again. You will laugh in amazement, laugh in gratitude, and laugh at the goodness of God.

Today I choose to laugh.
I may have gone through a tough season, but that was just a season.
This is my time to laugh!

TODAY I CHOOSE

To Keep an Eternal Perspective

I press on to reach the end of the race and receive the heavenly prize for which God, through Christ Jesus, is calling us.
Philippians 3:14 (NLT)

I heard a story once about a missionary couple who had spent over sixty years in Africa. They had given their lives to helping others and had done so much good. Now they were returning home to New York to retire. It just so happened they were booked on the same ship as President Teddy Roosevelt, who was returning home from one of his big hunting expeditions.

When the ship pulled into the dock, there was major fanfare. A band was playing. The mayor and other dignitaries were there. There were signs and balloons. When the president disembarked from the ship, the crowd went wild. Tens of thousands of people were cheering and waving. All the major newspapers were there taking photographs.

The missionary husband was very discouraged. He said to his wife, "It doesn't seem right. We've given our lives in service of others. We've done our best to make a difference.

Yet nobody even knows we exist. But he goes on vacation and the whole world welcomes him home."

Later that night, the man was praying. He said, "God, I don't understand. He returns with the fanfare of the world. We return, and nobody even knows we're here." He heard God say to him, down in his spirit, "Son, it's because you're not home yet."

Many of you have been faithful. You've sacrificed, volunteered, given all that you have. Know this: you will be rewarded. There will be a celebration like you've never seen. It won't be with a band you've ever heard of — the angels will be singing and all of Heaven will join in to welcome you home.

Be encouraged today. God sees every act of kindness. He sees every good deed. Nothing you've done has gone unnoticed. God saw it, and you will be rewarded. Choose today to keep an eternal perspective.

Today I choose to keep an eternal perspective. I won't worry about being rewarded here on earth. I will focus on what God has called me to do here because Heaven is my reward.

TODAY I CHOOSE

To Be Courageous

"This is my command—be strong and courageous! Do not be afraid or discouraged. For the LORD *your God is with you wherever you go."*
Joshua 1:9 (NLT)

There was a man in Scripture named Bartimaeus who had been blind since birth. Every day, he sat on the side of the road, begging and asking people for money. One day, there seemed to be a lot of extra commotion. Bartimaeus asked what was going on. The people said, "This teacher named Jesus is passing by."

Bartimaeus had heard about this Jesus and how He performed miracles, healing the sick and giving sight to the blind. So, Bartimaeus started shouting, *"Jesus, Son of David, have mercy on me!"* (Mark 10:47, NLT). Again and again, Bartimaeus shouted. The people around him started to object. *"Be quiet!"* they yelled at Bartimaeus, "You are causing a scene!" But Scripture says, *He only shouted louder* (v. 48, NLT).

Eventually, Jesus heard the shouting. He heard Bartimaeus's voice above all the others, and He said, *"Tell him to come here"* (v. 49, NLT). The people were incredulous. Jesus wasn't mad; He was about to do a miracle. When the people told Bartimaeus that Jesus was calling for him, Bartimaeus threw off his beggar's cloak, jumped up, and immediately went to Jesus. *"What do you want me to do for you?" Jesus asked. "My Rabbi," the blind man said, "I want to see!" And Jesus said to him, "Go, for your faith has healed you." Instantly the man could see* (vv. 51–52, NLT).

Bartimaeus was healed because he had a bold, courageous spirit. There were most likely lots of others on the road that day who needed favor, who needed breakthroughs, who were sick and even blind, but Bartimaeus was the one who stood out. Bartimaeus was the one who had the courage to shout — and to keep shouting — when everyone else told him to stay in his place.

God commands us to be courageous (Joshua 1:9). He wants you to release your faith for more. Start pursuing what God put in your heart. Don't shrink back; be courageous!

Today I choose to be courageous.
God has not given me a spirit of fear!

TODAY I CHOOSE

My Battles

Avoiding a fight is a mark of honor;
only fools insist on quarreling.
Proverbs 20:3 (NLT)

You are not supposed to engage in every conflict that presents itself to you. Only fools do that! It is easy to get baited into conflict, to argue with people and try to prove your point, but you have to be selective about which battles you fight.

Most of the things that come against us are simply distractions. If that battle is not between you and your destiny, you should ignore it. Ask yourself: *If I win this battle, what does it accomplish? How is it going to benefit me? Does it move me forward into my destiny?*

If someone is rude to you and you are rude back, your flesh may feel good, but it doesn't put you further down the road. If you spend your time trying to convince people to like you, what have you gained? You need to choose your battles wisely. If you make the mistake of engaging in every conflict, you're not going to have time for the battles that do matter.

When Nehemiah was rebuilding the walls of Jerusalem, there were two men who didn't like him. They were constantly criticizing him, spreading rumors, and trying to ruin his reputation. All day long they shouted insults, but Nehemiah just ignored them. He didn't get upset. He didn't try to straighten them out. He recognized that they were just a distraction. If he had wasted his time arguing with them, he wouldn't have built the walls in record time (Nehemiah 4–6).

When God puts a dream in your heart, there will always be people who are jealous, people who try to discredit you, who criticize you, and who try to get you riled up. That's not a battle you have to fight. God will strengthen you for the battles that are yours, but most of the battles will just be distractions that will get you off course and keep you from your destiny instead of moving you closer to it. Those are not battles you have to fight.

Today I choose my battles.
If it doesn't move me forward into my destiny, I will walk away.
It's not my battle to fight.

TODAY I CHOOSE

Long-Term Blessings over Short-Term Pleasure

No discipline seems pleasant at the time, but painful. Later on, however, it produces a harvest of righteousness and peace for those who have been trained by it.
Hebrews 12:11 (NIV)

Moses was born into a Hebrew family, but he was raised in the palace by the Pharaoh's daughter. He grew up with prestige and influence. However, as a young man, he saw how the Egyptians were oppressing the Hebrews, enslaving and mistreating them. He knew it wasn't right, and he chose to stand with the people of God.

In the palace, Moses had it made. He had wealth, influence, an easy life. But God had long-term blessings in store for him that required Moses to say no to what was easy now in favor of what was best in his future.

Like Moses, if you are going to reach the fullness of your destiny, there will be times you have to refuse things now that are less than God's best. Refuse the addictions that give you a short-term fix now if you want freedom in your future. Refuse unforgiveness now if you don't want it to poison your life later. Refuse to compromise now if you want promotion down the road.

Had Moses chosen to stay in his comfortable position in the palace, he never would have had his burning bush moment. He never would have brought the Israelites out of slavery, seen the Red Sea part, or watched his enemies drown in the water.

Hebrews 12:11 says, *No discipline seems pleasant at the time, but painful. Later on, however, it produces a harvest of righteousness and peace* (NIV). There will be things that you need to do that aren't fun, that are hard, and that your flesh won't like it. But you need to focus on the "later on." Focus on the reward. Focus on the greater things that God has in your future. The pain of discipline is less than the pain of regret. It may be difficult to say no now, but the reward will be worth it.

Today I choose long-term blessings over short-term pleasure. I don't need instant gratification; I need God's plan for my life.

TODAY I CHOOSE

To Believe the Best Is Yet to Come

"Your beginnings will seem humble,
so prosperous will your future be."
Job 8:7 (NIV)

In John 2, Jesus was at a wedding at Cana in Galilee. It was a huge celebration with hundreds of people in attendance. Everything was going great until they ran out of wine. Jesus' mother came and told Him about the problem. Jesus had not performed any miracles in public up to this point, but His mother knew something about Jesus that others didn't yet. She told the staff to do whatever Jesus asked them to do.

There were six large water pots nearby that held thirty gallons each. Jesus told the staff, *"Fill the jars with water"* (v. 7, NLT). Once they were filled, Jesus said, *"Now dip some out, and take it to the master of ceremonies"* (v. 8, NLT). When the master of the banquet had tasted the water-turned-wine, he called the groom over and said, *"Everybody I know begins with their finest wines and after the guests have had their fill brings in the cheap stuff. But you've saved the best till now!"* (v. 10, MSG).

What felt like a disaster — running out of wine at a wedding — was actually God removing what was good (the original wine) to make room for what was best (the miracle wine). God works in your life this way too. The relationship that felt fine suddenly is no longer working. God is removing what may have been good at first so that He can bring you the relationship that is best. The company you thought you'd work for forever suddenly shuts down. It's not a disaster. It's God moving you into something better.

Don't be discouraged when the wine runs out. God is about to open doors for you that you could never have opened on your own. He is moving you from good to best, sickness to health, fine to fabulous, restless to the peace that passes understanding. God's greatest feats are not in your yesterdays; they are always in your future.

Today I choose to believe the best is yet to come. My best days are not behind me; each day is better than the last.

TODAY I CHOOSE

To Receive God's Forgiveness

If we confess our sins, he is faithful and just to forgive us our sins and to cleanse us from all unrighteousness.
1 John 1:9 (ESV)

When Jesus was about to be crucified, He said to Peter, *"This very night, before the rooster crows, you will deny three times that you even know me"* (Matthew 26:34, NLT). Peter said, "No, Jesus. Even if everyone else does, I won't. Even if I have to die, I won't deny you." They arrested Jesus. Peter was watching it all take place from a distance. A young lady came over and pointed at Peter and said, "This man was with Jesus." Three times Peter denied it, and right on cue, the rooster crowed. When he realized what had happened, the Scripture says, Peter *went out and wept bitterly* (v. 75, NKJV).

Not long after that, they crucified Jesus. We've all made mistakes. We've all failed. But none of us have failed as big as Peter. None of us have denied Christ when He needed us the most, when He was about to be crucified.

On the third day, Mary went to the tomb to check on Jesus' body. When she arrived, an angel appeared and said,

"Do not be alarmed. You seek Jesus of Nazareth, who was crucified. He is risen! He is not here. See the place where they laid Him. But go, tell His disciples—and Peter—that He is going before you into Galilee" (Mark 16:6–7, NKJV).

Out of all the people in the world God could have mentioned at this historic time, the only person He specifically named was Peter. Just like God specifically called Peter's name, He is calling your name today, and He is saying, "Tell John, tell William, tell Ricardo, tell Shannon, tell Maria . . . I have forgiven them. I am not disappointed in them. I am not withholding My blessing. I still have an amazing future in front of them. You may have lost faith in me, but I haven't lost faith in you."

Today I choose to receive God's forgiveness. He knows all of my mistakes, and He chooses me anyway. I don't deserve it, but I choose to receive what He freely gives.

TODAY I CHOOSE

To Make a Generational Difference

But Ruth replied, "Don't ask me to leave you and turn back. Wherever you go, I will go; wherever you live, I will live. Your people will be my people, and your God will be my God."
Ruth 1:16 (NLT)

We all know what an amazing leader King David was, that he was "a man after God's own heart" (1 Samuel 13:14), but do you ever wonder how he got to be that way? I believe it's because his great-grandparents chose to make a generational difference.

If you go back three generations, David's great-grandparents were Ruth and Boaz. Ruth's first husband died at a young age, and she became a widow. Her mother-in-law, Naomi, became bitter after losing her own husband and both her sons. She decided to move back home to Bethlehem and told Ruth to go back to her father's house in Moab. But Ruth insisted on going with Naomi and making sure she was cared for. She left behind everything, including the idols that she had previously worshipped, and she made Naomi's God — the one true God — her God as well.

Every morning, Ruth would go to the fields and gather wheat so that she and Naomi could survive. Despite all the loss and heartache, she believed that God was in control, and God showed her favor by leading her to Boaz's field. Boaz was wealthy and influential, but more importantly, Boaz was kind and honorable. He made sure that Ruth and Naomi had more than enough.

Ruth and Boaz ended up getting married. They had a son named Obed, who had a son named Jesse, who had a son named David. No wonder David was so strong, confident, and full of faith. He could trace that faith back through his family line.

When you keep faith in God, that faith is not only impacting you and making your life better, but it is being transferred to your children and your grandchildren and your great-grandchildren. Every time you stand strong, every time you do the right thing when it's hard, every time you believe in your dreams even though circumstances are against you, you are making a generational difference.

Today I choose to make a generational difference. I will follow God faithfully and leave the next generation a legacy of faith!

TODAY I CHOOSE

To Commit My Way to the Lord

Delight yourself also in the LORD, and He shall give you the desires of your heart. Commit your way to the LORD, trust also in Him, and He shall bring it to pass.
Psalm 37:4–5 (NKJV)

When the Scripture says, *He shall give you the desires of your heart*, we might read that to mean God will give us whatever we want, but another perspective is: when you honor God, He will put the right desires in you. When you've committed your ways to Him, He will make sure you have the right desires in your heart, and He'll make sure those things happen.

Sometimes life can be confusing. We wonder what our purpose is, what we are supposed to do, which path to take, which city to live in, which college to attend, or which degree to choose. Scripture says that *God is not the author of confusion but of peace* (1 Corinthians 14:33, NKJV). He wants you to have peace in decision-making and peace when it comes to knowing His plan. If you don't have peace, you aren't trusting Him. You haven't committed all your ways to Him.

Knowing God's will for our lives is not as difficult as we make it. If you're keeping Him first and committing all your ways to Him, there will be things that you are passionate about, things that you're gifted at, opportunities that excite you, and dreams that motivate you. That is God leading you into your destiny.

God says in Psalm 32:8, *"I will guide you along the best pathway for your life. I will advise you and watch over you"* (NLT). When God is leading you, you don't have to worry about missing your destiny. He's going to override wrong decisions. He's going to close doors you're not supposed to go through. He's going to move people out who shouldn't be there. You don't have to worry about following the wrong path. You can follow what He puts in your heart. When you've committed your ways to Him, you can be confident He is putting the right desires in you.

Today I choose to commit my way to the Lord. I trust that He will put desires in my heart that line up with His.

TODAY I CHOOSE

To Be a Blessing

Jesus said to them, My food (nourishment) is to do the will (pleasure) of Him Who sent Me and to accomplish and completely finish His work.
John 4:34 (AMPC)

After Jesus and the disciples had traveled a long way to Samaria, they were tired and hungry. Jesus sent the disciples into town to get food while He waited at the well. He met a woman, told her about her future, and gave her a new beginning.

The disciples came back a few hours later with food, but Jesus wasn't hungry anymore. The disciples were surprised. They tried to offer him something to eat, but He wouldn't take it. He said, *"I have food to eat that you know nothing about"* (John 4:32, NIV). They thought somebody must have come while they were gone and given Jesus something to eat. How could He be tired one minute and refreshed the next? Jesus told them the secret. He said, *"My food is to do the will of him who sent me and to accomplish his work"* (John 4:34, ESV). Jesus was saying, "I get fed by doing what God wants me to do, by doing what pleases Him. I get nourished when I help people. My strength, peace, joy, and satisfaction come when I serve others."

You can work all day, and, in the natural, you'll get tired. But after a long, tiring day, you can go out of your way to be a blessing — to serve at a local soup kitchen, mow your neighbor's lawn, or stop by the hospital — and you will go home stronger and refreshed. Some people spend the whole weekend doing nothing, trying to "rest up" for another work week and still wake up tired on Monday morning. But others get up early to serve their church and stay up late watching a friend's kids so they can have a date night with their spouse, and, by serving others, by doing what God has called and equipped them to do, they get fed. What should wear them out fills them up, because when you do the will of your Father, it doesn't drain you; it replenishes you.

Today I choose to be a blessing. When I do the will of the Father, I am filled up.

TODAY I CHOOSE

The Abundant Life

"It is a land where food is plentiful and nothing is lacking. It is a land where iron is as common as stone, and copper is abundant in the hills."
Deuteronomy 8:9 (NLT)

When the Israelites were in slavery in Egypt for four hundred years, that was the land of "not enough." There was no freedom. They were barely surviving, enduring slave labor and harsh punishments, barely making it through.

One day, God brought them out of slavery and took them into the desert. That was the land of "just enough." Their needs were supplied but nothing more. They had food for one day at a time and tents to shelter them at night but nothing extra. No changes of clothing. No food to store up to give them a sense of security.

After forty years, God eventually took the Israelites into the Promised Land. That was the land of "more than enough." The food and supplies were plentiful. The bundles of grapes were so big it took two people to carry them. It was called the land flowing with milk and honey. Flowing means it never stopped. It didn't dry up. There was always an abundance.

That's where God is taking you — to the abundant life.

By now you know that you choose your thoughts. Therefore, all through the day, you can choose to meditate on thoughts of God and the abundant life He has for you. Meditate on thoughts of overflow, on more than enough. Say, "As He did for the Israelites, God takes pleasure in prospering me."

You may be in the land of "not enough" right now. Don't worry. God hasn't forgotten about you. Maybe you're in the land of "just enough." You're grateful that your needs are supplied, but there's no extra. There's nothing to accomplish your dreams. Those are seasons, and the good news is they are not permanent. You are passing through. God has a promised land for you. He has a place of abundance, of "more than enough."

Today I choose the abundant life. God did not breathe life into me to give me just enough to get by. He has a place of abundance, of more than enough, for me, and that is where I choose to dwell!

TODAY I CHOOSE

Jesus

Have you made Jesus the Lord of your life? Pray this simple prayer with me:

> *"Lord Jesus, I repent of my sins.*
> *I ask You to come into my heart.*
> *I make You my Lord and Savior."*

If you prayed that simple prayer, you have been born again. Get in a good Bible-based church. Keep God first place in your life. Today and every day, choose Jesus!

ABOUT JOEL OSTEEN MINISTRIES

Joel Osteen Ministries, rooted in Houston, Texas, is an extension of the legacy built by John and Dodie Osteen, who founded Lakewood Church in 1959. Originally meeting in a modest feed store, Lakewood has grown into one of the largest congregations in the US, attracting people from all walks of life. John Osteen's leadership touched millions through his television ministry, which reached over 100 countries, and his influence as a pastor's pastor. His wife, Dodie, also played a key role, especially with her testimony of miraculous healing from cancer, which has inspired countless people.

When John passed away in 1999, his son Joel stepped into leadership, despite his background in television production. Joel's transition into senior pastor marked a new era for Lakewood, with the church's global influence expanding significantly. Under Joel's leadership, Lakewood's outreach grew, broadcasting to over 200 million households, and the church became a beacon of hope for millions seeking encouragement and inspiration.

Joel's wife, Victoria, serves alongside him, contributing to the church's leadership and vision. Their daughter, Alexandra, continues the family tradition, leading worship and contributing to Lakewood Music. With a focus on uplifting messages and practical teachings, Joel Osteen Ministries aims to reach new generations, inspiring people worldwide to rise above their challenges and live their best life through faith, hope, and love.